SPALDING.

Winning Tennis

Chuck Kriese

MASTERS PRESS

A Division of Howard W. Sams & Co.

Published by Masters Press (A Division of Howard W. Sams & Co.)
2647 Waterfront Parkway E. Dr.
Suite 300
Indianapolis, IN 46214

First printing, March 1993.
Second printing, April, 1993.
Third printing, June 1994.

Printed in the United States of America

Library of Congress Cataloging-in-Publication Data
Kriese, Chuck 1950-
Winning Tennis / by Chuck Kriese.
p. cm. — (Spalding sports library)
ISBN 0-940279-61-4:
1. Tennis—Training. I. Title. II. Series.
GV995.K75 1993 93-6698
796.342'2—dc20 CIP

Credits

Editor: Mark Montieth

Cover Design: Lynne Clark

Illustrations: Lynne Clark

Cover photograph: Nancy Gilstrap, *Anderson Independent*, Anderson, S.C.

Inside photographs: Russ Adams, Bob Waldrop, Scott Harkey, Scott Craft, Clemson Sports Information Department

Models: Paul Kruse, Kris Huff, Joe Defoor, Richard Matuszewski

Table of Contents

To the Kriese boys, Clay, Adam, and John,
whom I love unconditionally and forever.

To my loving wife, Cheryl,
for her great help and support throughout this project.

✝

Preface

I've often wondered why the great Jack Kramer titled his book *The Game*. I strongly believe that it was out of respect.

You have decided to learn to play the best game ever invented. The simplicity of the game is beautiful to see at the beginning levels, and the multiple dimensions at the highest levels are almost too many to discuss. The game of tennis can test every part of your inner and outer self, but it also can be as relaxing as a walk in the afternoon sun. It can bring moments of elation and satisfaction as well as periods of frustration and disappointment. It can be played by people of any age or skill level, but it can never be mastered. Therefore, the emphasis must be on enjoyment.

One of my rookie players once told me after a practice that "the more that I learn about tennis, the more that I find out I don't know about the game." I replied that the best perspective for him to take was to submit to it, completely out of respect, and play it as hard as he could; just be totally honored to be a competitor within it.

Tennis cannot be conquered, and it will not serve your means for status, fame, or fortune. To be a part of it, however, is a great happening. Tennis truly is "the sport of a lifetime."

Chris Evert burst on to the national tennis scene early, and stayed a long time.

*"Remove not the ancient landmark,
which the fathers have set."*

— Old Testament, Proverbs

1

Tenez, Anyone?

Tennis originated during the days of the early Romans and Greeks. They played a game with a ball made up of cloth stripping wrapped with twine. The French also played an indoor court game called *jeu de peume* ("game of the palm") which was played with the hands before a crude type of racquet was used starting about 1300.

This court game evolved and became quite popular in France and England. In the 19th century, it became known as *tenez*, meaning "take it, play."

The man known as the father and inventor of lawn tennis was Major Walter Wingfield. He took aspects of badminton and inside court tennis and used racquets for his game called *sphairistike*. His first courts were shaped like an hour glass and had nets seven feet high. He patented a portable court and net for his game, and it blossomed in popularity about 1875.

The All-England Croquet Club (Wimbledon) changed its lawns to tennis courts during this period and the play was so popular that it rescued the club from financial trouble.

At about the same time, Mary Outerbridge, while vacationing in Bermuda, witnessed the game being played by a friend of Major Wingfield. She brought the ideas and the game back to New York and convinced the Staten Island Cricket Club to construct courts. For five years the game grew in popularity until it became necessary to have a meeting among the New York clubs to determine standards for rules, equipment, and courts. In May of 1881, the USLTA (United States Lawn Tennis Association) was formed.

Dr. James Dwight became the first president of the USLTA and held that office for 21 years. He is known as the father of American tennis. Interest continued to grow, and in 1900 Dr. Dwight Davis donated a cup (the Davis Cup) that would be used as a trophy for competition between the U.S. and England each year. This competition later became a world-wide event, and today the Davis Cup is among the most coveted of international trophies.

Mrs. George Wightman donated a similar trophy in 1923 for women's international competition, the Wightman Cup. In 1962, the Federation Cup was inaugurated and became a standard for women's international competition.

Champions and Trend Setters

Tennis in the 20th century has been influenced by many great players, some of whom have become legends. They dominated the four grand slam events: Wimbledon, the U.S. Open, the French Open, and the Australian Open. Many other outstanding personalities have made contributions to the sport.

Early champions

Richard Sears. The first U.S. Nationals Champion, from 1882-87.

William (Little Bill) Johnson. The U.S. Nationals Champion in 1915 and 1919. With his unorthodox strokes, heavy western freehand grip and all-court game, he controlled early battles against "Big Bill" Tilden.

William (Big Bill) Tilden. Considered by many the greatest player of all time, and definitely the greatest of the early 20th centry. A master of every shot, this man of tall physical stature dominated the game during the "Golden Age of Sport," much like Babe Ruth, Red Grange and Jack Dempsey dominated their respective sports. He became famous for playing to his opponents' strengths instead of their weaknesses in order to dismantle their confidence during matches.

Rene La Coste and **Henry Cochet.** La Coste won the U.S. Nationals in 1926 and '27, and Cochet won in 1928. These Frenchmen were consistent counter-punchers who used placement and control of spins as their strengths.

Ellsworth Vines. A California native who used a power game to win the U.S. Nationals in 1931 and '32.

Fred Perry. This Englishman was the U.S. Nationals Champion in 1933, '34 and '36. His great court speed, flat continental forehand and confident approach made him the sport's dominant player until Don Budge emerged.

Don Budge. Thought by some to have the greatest backhand of all time, Budge was the first winner of the Grand Slam, winning the U.S. Nationals, Wimbledon, the French National and the Australian National in 1938. He made up for his lack of speed by playing closer to the net and taking balls early, thus forcing his opponent into a defensive positon.

Bobby Riggs. One of the game's best mental strategists and a true "player" of tennis. He used clever tactics and deceptive shot-making to beat many bigger and stronger opponents. He won the U.S. Nationals in 1939 and '41, but probably is best known today for his "Battle of the Sexes" matches against Margaret Court and Billy Jean King in the 1970s.

Jack Kramer. The U.S. Nationals champion in 1946 and '47, who popularized the serve and volley game, which became known as "The Big Game." He later played professionally on an eight-player circuit against the likes of Riggs and the younger, big-hitting Pancho Gonzales.

Pancho Gonzalez. At 6 foot, 3 inches, this U.S. Nationals champion of 1948 and '49 was one of the most outstanding athletes ever to play the game. His serve was clocked at 118 miles per hour, which was unprecedented in the era of the smaller, wooden racquet frame. He turned pro in 1949.

Doris Hart. A U.S. Wightman Cup great, she won Wimbledon in 1951 and won the U.S. Nationals at Forest Hills in 1954 and '55. She won numerous Grand Slam titles in the 1940's and 1950's.

Maureen Connolly Brinker. Known as "Little Mo," she won the U.S. Nationals from 1951-53. She never lost in Wightman Cup competition, and was the first woman to win the Grand Slam in 1953. Her career was cut short by a freak accident while horseback riding.

Althea Gibson. Considered the first great black women's champion. She won Wimbledon and the U.S. Nationals in 1957 and '58. She later went on to a successful professional golf career.

Tony Trabert. Champion of the U.S. Nationals in 1953 and '55. A fierce competitor known for his great backhand volley, he turned professional in 1955 after gaining fame as the world's best amateur player. He later became a well-known television analyst for tennis events.

Ken Rosewall. Standing only 5 foot, 7 inches, he was called "Muscles" by his coach, Harry Hopman, because of his strength and stamina. His backhand was perhaps the most perfect of all tennis strokes. He became one of the key performers in a group of Australian greats who dominated the Davis Cup for nearly 20 years under Hopman. Rosewall won the U.S. Nationals in 1957 and '60 as well as many other Grand Slam titles.

Roy Emerson. A steady performer recognized as the best doubles player of his era. He won the U.S. Nationals in 1961 and '64 and helped Australia to many Davis Cup Titles. Had great speed and competitiveness.

Rod Laver. Nicknamed "The Rocket," he was a left-handed master of speed and shot-making. Along with Rosewall, Emerson, Stolle, Newcombe, Fraser and others, Laver helped Australia dominate the Davis Cup during the 1950's and '60's. He became the only man to win the Grand Slam twice, in 1962 and '69. John McEnroe said he based his style of play on Laver's style.

Chuck McKinley. Ranked among the top five in the world from 1962-64, he was the Wimbledon singles champion in 1963 and won the U.S. Nationals in doubles with Dennis Ralston in 1961, '63 and '64.

Dennis Ralston. Teamed with McKinley to win the Davis Cup doubles titles, and was ranked in the top 10 in the world seven times in 1960's. He went on to coach collegiate tennis at Southern Methodist University.

Modern-day champions

Before 1969, the professional tennis circuit consisted of a few players traveling from one site to another with their own schedule of events. The Grand Slam events and other championships were for amateurs.

In 1969, however, tennis became an "open" sport, meaning the major tournaments were opened to pros and amateurs alike, and most events on the tour began offering prize money. This change in the structure of the sport led to the "tennis boom" of the 1970's, as the sport gained widespread popularity around the world. Tennis grew faster during this 10-year period than at any other time in its history.

Billy Jean King. Probably the most influential figure in women's tennis. She was the first female tennis player to earn $100,000 in one season, and was named Athlete of the Year by the Associated Press in 1967 and 1973 and Sportswoman of the Year by *Sports Illustrated* magazine in 1972. She won a record 20 Wimbledon titles.

Arthur Ashe. Another star player whose impact transcended the game. The first great black American player, he won the U.S. Open championship as an amateur during the transitional year of 1968. He was ranked No. 1 in the world in 1968 and '75, and won the Australian Open in 1970 and Wimbledon in 1975. A former U.S. Davis Cup coach, Ashe was one of greatest worldwide ambassadors for the sport.

Chris Evert. One of the greatest women's champions of all time. She burst onto the tennis scene at 16, reaching the U.S. Open semi-finals in 1971, and was a consistent winner until her retirement in 1990. In addition to her many Grand Slam titles, she is greatly respected for her consistency and longevity as a champion and her impeccable court demeanor. She perfected the flawless baseline style that hundreds of American girls emulated.

Stan Smith. An American Davis Cup great of the 1970s and the 1972 Wimbldon champion. He was ranked No. 1 in the U.S. in 1969, '71, '72 and '73. As a coach, he guided the USTA National Team to world prominence in the late 1980s and early 1990s.

Bjorn Borg. Perhaps the greatest impact player in the post-war era. He turned professional as a teenager in 1973 after dominating the world's Junior Tour. The Swede was one of the first modern players to use the two-handed backhand and heavy, looping strokes. His style influenced thousands of players as he went on to win five consecutive Wimbledon titles from 1976-'80. His influence brought Sweden to the forefront as a world tennis power.

Jimmy Connors. Considered by many the 20th century's "ultimate warrior of tennis." His longevity and competitiveness have set the standard for toughness. A former NCAA champion, he won the U.S. Open in 1974, '76, '78

The influence of Arthur Ashe transcended the world of tennis.

and '82. He won Wimbledon in 1974 and '82, and he was ranked No. 1 in the world from 1974-'78. He holds the record for most Grand Prix titles.

Martina Navratilova. The most athletic of the women champions, this serve-and-volley attacking player set the record for the most Grand Prix titles for women. Her dramatic matches with Chris Evert for dominance of the women's circuit were known for their drama and contrast of styles.

John McEnroe. A United States Davis Cup great in the 1980s, he won the U.S. Open in 1979, '80, '81, and '84, and won Wimbledon in 1981, '83 and '84. Recognized as one of greatest competitors of all time, he dominated tennis along with Borg and Connors in the late 1970s and throughout the 1980s.

Ivan Lendl. One of the most consistent champions from the 1980s and 90s, he is known for physical fitness and mental toughness. He battled McEnroe and Connors for many titles, and won the U.S. Open in 1985, '86, and '87.

Boris Becker. The youngest Wimbledon champion of all time, winning the title in 1987 at age 17. He was the first of the modern German champions.

Stefan Edberg. This great Swedish champion won the U.S. Open in 1991 and '92, and was ranked No. 1 in the world during that time. Unlike the other Swedish great, Bjorn Borg, he played an attacking serve-and-volley game.

Special contributors

Bud Collins. An award-winning journalist for the *Boston Globe* and later a television commentator, his colorful and flamboyant style helped bring tennis to the masses in the 1970s and '80s.

Dennis Van Der Meer. Recognized as one of world's greatest teachers from the 1960s through the '90s. He also is the founder of the United States Professional Tennis Registry (USPTR), through which hundreds of leading professional have trained. Author of hundreds of articles and several books, he has had a profound effect on the world of tennis, primarily because of his longevity and consistent devotion to excellence.

Harry Hopman. Recognized as "the greatest coach of all time" by *Tennis* magazine. A former Australian playing great and sportswriter, he is most remembered for coaching the dominant Australian Davis Cup teams that included players such as Laver, Rosewall, Fred Stolle, Lew Hoad, Neale Frasier, Emerson and John Newcombe. He changed tennis from a country club sport with his tough training methods and trained many modern era champions, such as McEnroe, Peter Fleming and Mary Carillo.

Jimmy Van Allen. A champion player, inventor and innovator. Van Allen founded the International Lawn Tennis Hall of Fame at Newport in 1954 and was the originator of the tie-breaker system and of no-ad scoring, which was widely used in collegiate tennis in the 1980s.

Howard Head. Conceived, invented and developed the oversized racquet that became the standard. His large racquet, first regarded as a joke, was the most dramatic change in racquet design in the 20th century.

"Winning is not a sometime thing,
it's an all-time thing.
You don't win once in a while,
you don't do things right once in a while,
you do them right all the time.
Winning is a habit.
Unfortunately, so is losing."

— Vince Lombardi

2

Gearing Up to Play

Matches can be lost because of improper or inadequate equipment. Yet even at the highest levels of the game, players sometimes neglect to make sure they are properly equipped.

In 1980, for example, we had a match against a team ranked among the top 10 in the country. My No. 1 player, John, showed up with only two racquets, although I require my players to bring four to each match.

John explained that he had strung these two racquets the night before, and expected no problems. But in the third game, the racquet flew out of his hand as he served and broke, leaving him with one. Two games later, a string on that racquet broke. Suddenly I was running around the complex looking for a substitute racquet.

John was able to finish the match with a teammate's racquet, but the damage was done. He lost his match, and our team lost 5-4 in what could have been a great victory for us.

I was furious afterward. It was useless, I told my players, to train hard for big matches if simple details such as inadequate equipment, diet or sleep prevented us from winning. John went on to become an All-American, but learned an important lesson the hard way.

Not everyone can or should carry four racquets with them for every match, but it is important to find the racquet that best suits your needs. Likewise, you should have knowledge of the other equipment needed to play, including balls, shoes and clothing, and understand the rules and etiquette. You will play better, and enjoy the game more in the process.

What's Your Racquet?

Extra-wide, wide or normal body? Oversize or midsize head? Flexible or stiff shaft? Tight or loose string tension?

So many racquets are available now that even experienced players have difficulty choosing one. All manufacturers claim to have some special quality that makes theirs better than the others.

I advise getting help from a teaching pro or an experienced player. Then select an inexpensive or medium-priced racquet to start with. It is not necessary at first to have an expensive racquet; any sturdy racquet will do.

As your stroking skills improve, you will be in a better position to decide which size and type of racquet is best for you. As with your style of play, it must be your choice alone. A good choice cannot be made, however, without some playing experience.

Racquet types include the following:

Oversize racquet head. Howard Head invented, developed, and marketed the biggest equipment revolution in the history of tennis with his oversized racquet manufactured by Prince. Many considered the racquet a joke in the early 1980's, but within five years Prince cornered more than 50 percent of the market with the revolutionary racquet. Head's invention opened the door for manufacturers to experiment with sizes, materials and shapes for racquets.

The oversize racquet has forever changed tennis. Now, even the beginning player can keep balls in play as never before because of the larger "sweet spot," which is the center portion of the strings with which the player tries to strike the ball. The obvious advantage of the oversize racquet is that you can play a more consistent game at every level.

Midsize racquet head. This is probably the most popular racquet for the tour player, because it has a generous sweet spot but still enables the player to generate better racquet head speed and power. Professional players can perform as consistently with a midsize racquet as with an oversized racquet, but the oversize racquet remains the more practical tool for the beginner.

Wide body frame. These enable the player to generate more power as the ball leaves the racquet strings more quickly. This type of frame, however, makes it more difficult to generate spin and to control the ball. Players must weigh their need for power and control when selecting this racquet.

Medium-width frame. These enable moderate power, but improve control. They are preferred by most professionals. Smaller heads, once the only size available, are not used commonly.

Flexible racquet shafts. These absorb most of the shock of the hit, but enable less power. They are easiest on the player's arm, but the flex in the shaft may take time to get accustomed to.

Stiff racquet shafts. These are made of substances such as graphite, aluminum and boron, and although they supply more power, the shaft does not absorb as much of the shock from striking the ball. Players sometimes complain of extra stress put on the arm with stiff racquets.

Loose strings. Loose string tension gives more power to the player, but detracts from control.

Tight strings. Tight strings give less power, because of the decreased elasticity, but enable more control.

Stepping into the Right Shoes

As with racquets, a wide variety of shoes are available. The most important thing to remember is to choose smooth-soled tennis shoes designed for court play. It is a mistake, as well as a breach of etiquette, to play in basketball shoes or black-soled shoes, both of which can leave marks on the tennis court and damage the surface. Wear the most comfortable shoes you can find. Your feet are probably your most important resource on the tennis court. Take care of them!

Having a Ball

Tennis balls are basically all alike, with only a few differences. The cover of the ball should be resilient and the air pressure inside should make it hard. Basically, two or three companies monopolize the sale of balls, so they are very uniform.

Balls are packaged in pressurized cans by the manufacturers. When you open the can, you should hear a hiss. The cover on the ball is either heavy-duty felt for play on hard courts, or regular-duty for clay. The heavier duty felt enables more control, and therefore longer rallies between players. On clay courts, heavy duty balls tend to become too heavy and difficult to hit with pace. Playing experience quickly teaches you the difference.

Dressing for Class and Comfort

Some clubs and organizations have special dress codes, such as requiring white collared shirts, or tennis dresses for women. Most places are more flexible today, as long as the clothes are not extremely radical. Your main concern should be comfort and appropriateness. Choose clothes that breathe, preferably at least 50 percent natural fabric. Most players wear heavy socks, or even two pairs to protect the feet. Special tennis socks that provide extra cushion for toes and heels are available. Again, your feet may be your most important resource.

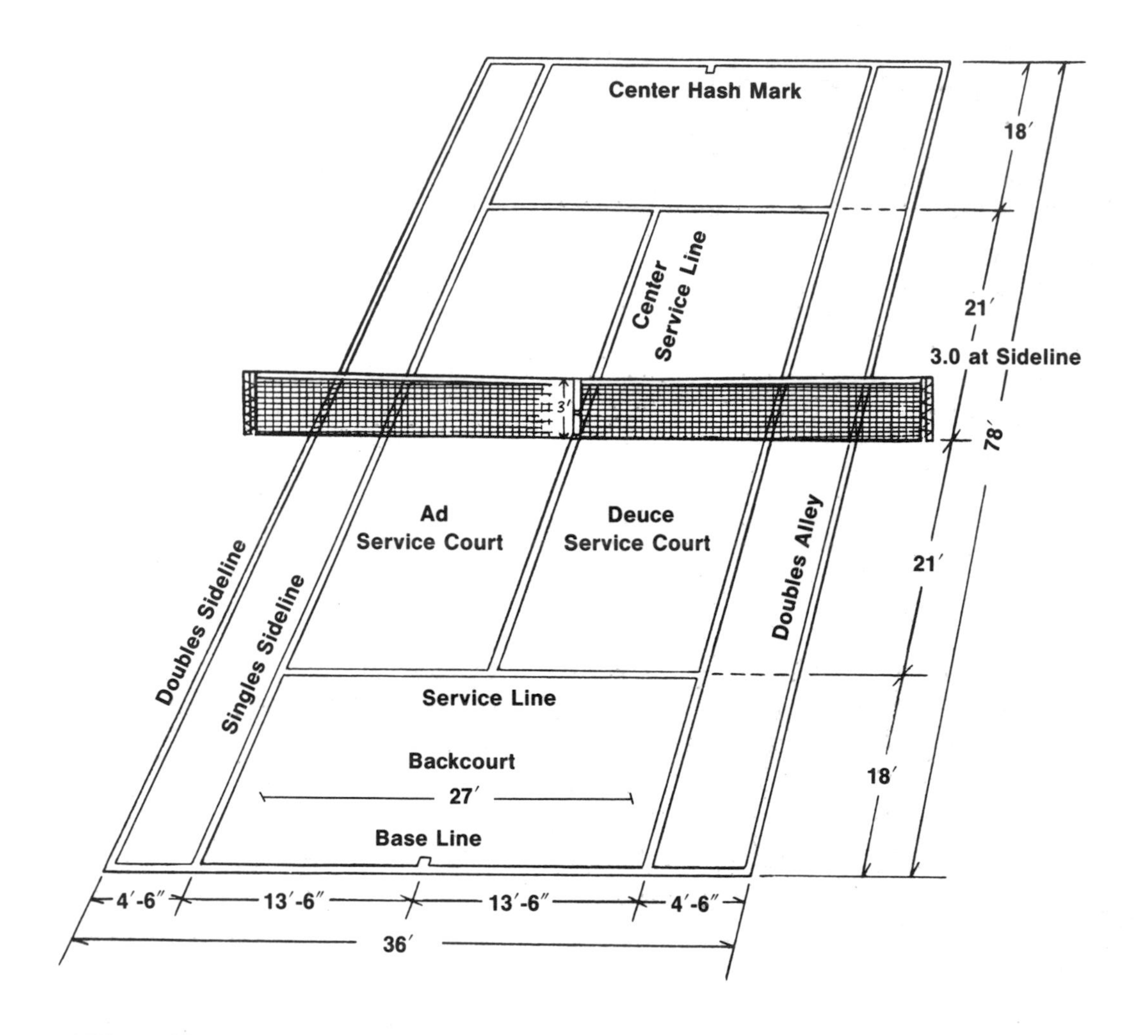

The Court

Tennis can be played indoors or outdoors, and on courts made of anything from grass to wood to cement. Each type of surface has its unique characteristics.

Hard courts. These are made of asphalt, wood, cement, or composition materials. They give a consistent and reliable bounce with a minimum amount of maintenance, but they can be hard on your feet and legs and reflect heat. If it is really hot, then you will be too. Hard courts are the most common because of their ease of care.

Soft courts. These are usually made of clay or a man-made substance called Har-Tru. They provide a much slower and higher bounce, and are easiest on the legs. They can be more fun to play, particularly for beginners, because the ball does not bounce as fast. They can require a great deal of maintenance, however; they usually need to be watered, rolled and lined daily.

Grass courts. Grass courts are relatively uncommon because of the tremendous upkeep required to cut the grass and groom the courts. Grass was once the primary surface for play, but now is found only at the most exclusive clubs and few tournaments other than Wimbledon. The ball bounces very low and skids somewhat, making play on this surface very fast. Grass is very easy on the feet and the body and is the most beautiful surface of all courts.

Indoor courts. These can be made of many differenct surfaces. They generally are much faster-paced and are more pure for shot-making due to the lack of wind, sun, and other elements that affect play out of doors. Players should focus their strategy on hitting the ball harder, taking shots a step or two closer to the net and playing more aggressively.

Keeping Score

Tennis has a unique scoring system that sets it apart from any other sport. The use of units to score makes it exciting from start to finish, because the game is truly never "over until it is over." It would not be as intriguing with a mundane 1, 2, 3 scoring system.

Novice players quickly realize they must concentrate and play their best from start to finish. It is important to gain early momentum, but a player still can win a match by hanging in long enough to change the momentum. Advanced players learn how to manage momentum and match flow.

Units of scoring

A *match* consists of a maximum of three or five sets. The first player to win the best of three or the best of five wins the match.

A *set* consists of at least six games. A player must win by a margin of at least two games to win a set. A tie-breaker usually is played after each player wins six games. Set scores are 6-0, 6-1, 6-2, 6-3, 6-4 or 7-5, or 7-6 when the tie-breaker is used.

A *game* can be won by scoring a minimum of four points and gaining an advantage of at least two points.

The unique scoring method is as follows.

0 points — love

1 point — 15

2 points — 30

3 points — 40

4 points — game

If the opponents are tied at 3 or more points, the score is called *deuce*.

If one player is ahead by one point after the third point, the score is then called *advantage server* (ad in) or *advantage receiver* (ad out).

The *tie-breaker* system has become standardized after a period of experimentation. When the tie-breaker was first used, many different methods were tried. The two most popular were the nine-point sudden-death tie-breaker, in which the first player to score five points was the winner, and the first-to-seven, win-by-two, 12-point tie-breaker. The 12-point tie-breaker is now used exclusively in official competition.

In this system, the winner is the first player reach seven points with a margin of at least two points over the opponent. The first point is served into the deuce court (from the server's right-hand court to the opposite court). The opponent then serves point 2 to the ad court and point 3 to the deuce court. Points 4 and 5 are served to the ad court and deuce court, respectively, by the first server. The players continue to serve two at a time from each side of the court until one of the players scores seven points and leads by two points.

After every six-point interval (after the sixth point, after the 12th point, and so on) the players change ends of the court and continue the normal sequence. For example, after the sixth point has been played by serving to the ad court, the players change sides of the net and the seventh point is served by the same player into the deuce court.

Before the days of the tie-breaker, matches theoretically could go on forever, and some almost did. The record for most games played in a professional match is 112, in a first-round Wimbledon match in 1969. Pancho Gonzalez defeated Charlie Pasarell 22-24, 1-6, 16-14, 6-3, 11-9 in a match lasting five hours and 12 minutes. In Davis Cup competition, competitors still play out the entire set, without the use of tie-breakers.

Understanding Rules and Etiquette

The following are the basic rules and etiquette of tennis, as provided by the United States Tennis Association in its booklet, *Illustrated Introduction to the Rules of Tennis*.

Before a game

1. Talk quietly when standing near tennis courts that are in use.
2. Don't walk across the back of another court until the players have finished playing a point. This can be distracting to them.
3. If people are already on your court, don't disturb them until their time is up.
4. When you are ready to play, put racquet covers, ball cans, jackets and other gear out of everyone's way.
5. Wear sneakers. Other shoes may wear out quickly, hurt your feet or damage the court.

Starting a game

1. Learn the names of the lines and which ones are applicable to the game you are playing (singles or doubles).
2. To see who serves first, spin your racquet or toss a coin. If you win the toss, the choice is yours. You may serve first, or you may choose to receive first and pick which end of the court you want to begin play. As a third choice, you may make your opponent choose first.
3. To put the ball into play for each point, one player serves the ball from behind the baseline. That player is called the server; the other player is called the receiver.

Scoring

1. The first point won by a player is *15*. The other player with no points has *love*.
2. If the next point is won by the same player, the score is *30-love*.
3. If the same player wins the third and fourth points, the score is *40-love* and then the game is over.
4. If each player wins three points so that the game is tied 40- 40, the score is called *deuce*. The player who wins the next point as the *advantage*, often called *ad-in* for the server or *ad-out* for the receiver. If the same player wins the next point, the game is over. If not, the score goes back to deuce. The first player to score two points in a row after a deuce wins the game.
5. Call the score of the set (such as 4-3) before serving for the first point of the game. Call the game score just before serving for each point. The server's score is always said first.
6. The first player to win at least six games and to be ahead by at least two games win a *set*. The first one to win two sets win a *match*. If the score reaches six games all, you may play a tie-break game (*tie-breaker*). Whoever wins this game wins the set.

Serving

1. Before serving, be sure that the receiver is ready to play.
2. When serving the first point, stand behind the baseline between the center mark and the right side line. When serving, you are not allowed to step on or over the baseline before hitting the ball.
3. The first serve must go over the net into the receiver's right service court. If it does not, it is called a fault. You get a second chance.
4. If you serve a ball that hits the tape of the net before bouncing into the correct service court, it is called a *let*. You may take that serve again.

If it hits the net and then goes outside the service court, it is called a fault. A served ball hitting the post also is a fault.

5. When serving the next point, stand behind the baseline between the center mark and the left side line. The ball must go across the net into the receiver's left service court.
6. After you have served one game in a set, you switch ends of the court and then receive your opponent's serve for one game. You switch ends again after the third, fifth and every odd-numbered game.

Playing a point

1. Except when serving, you may stand anywhere — in or out of bounds — on your side of the net.
2. Except when receiving serve, you have the choice of hitting the ball on your side before it bounces, or after one bounce. The receiver must let the serve bounce once before hitting it.
3. You win the point if you hit the ball over the net into the court on the other side and your opponent does not return it.
4. A ball is still in play if it happens to touch the net or post.
5. Continue to play a ball that lands on our touches a boundary line of the court.
6. You lose the point if you hit the ball into the net or out of the court (unless your opponent volleys the outgoing ball).
7. You also lose the point if the ball touches you or your clothing, if you or your racquet touch the net or post, if you hit a ball before it passes the net, or if you deliberately hit the ball more than once. You're on your honor to make these calls against yourself.

Calling lines

1. If the ball touches any part of the line, it is good. Call the ball out only if you can clearly see a space between where the ball hits and the line.
2. It is your job to make any out calls immediately.
3. If you cannot see that a ball is definitely out, you should continue playing the point.
4. If later you see a mark on the court that indicates a ball you played was out, you cannot suddenly call it out. The point stands as played.
5. If a ball goes past you and you cannot see where it lands, you must give the point to your opponent.
6. You lose the point if you catch the ball on the fly, no matter where you think it might land and even if you are standing outside of the court.

Introduce yourself to your opponent before each match.

After the last point of the match, shake hands with your opponent.

Doubles

1. In doubles, you and a partner play against a team of two players on the other side of the net, using the full court from doubles side line to double side line. Either of you on the team serving first may begin the match. Either person on the opposing team may receive the first ball in the right (or deuce) court. When it is your team's turn to receive, you choose which player will play which court. You must then keep the same order of serving and the same sidese for receiving for the whole set.
2. If the server's partner is hit with the serve, a fault is called. If the receiver's partner is hit with the serve, the server wins the point.
3. In returning shots (except the serve), either member of a doubles team may hit the ball. The partners don't have to alternate hits.

Court conduct

1. Introduce yourself to your opponent.
2. Limit the warm-up before a match to approximately five minutes. Hit back and forth with your opponent and take a few practice serves.
3. You should help your partner with line calls when possible. If you think a ball that your partner has called out actually hit the line, you must call it good.
4. Keep a positive outlook on the game. Remember, you're playing for the fun of it.
5. Keep the game moving. Don't stall and waste time between points. Accept all calls made by your opponent, without arguing or sulking.
6. Don't distract your opponent on purpose by unnecessary movements or talking.
7. If a serve is out, don't return it if you can avoid doing so. Just tap it gently into the net or let it go behind you.
8. If your ball goes into the court, wait until the players finish the point before you ask for the ball. If a ball comes onto your court, return it as soon as play has stopped on both courts.
9. If there is any disagreement on the score, go back to the last score that you both can agree on, or spin a racquet.
10. After the last point of the match, come to the net quickly and shake hands. Let your opponent know that you appreciated the match, no matter what the outcome.

"If you want to win your battles,
take and work your bloomin' guns."

— Rudyard Kipling

3 Getting in Shape

If you are willing to invest some time working on your physical training, your game will improve greatly.

Your training program should address the following areas:

- Anaerobic endurance
- Flexibility strength
- Speed agility
- Nutrition
- Injury prevention and treatment

A rigorous and consistent program of physical training enhances a player's performance on the tennis court for the following reasons:

It increases confidence in match situations. A player who is prepared physically for a match will be prepared mentally as well, and mental preparation enables emotional comfort. An athlete who has trained diligently will think, "I have done all I can do and I'm ready to play." This enables the athlete to play the match without pressing, rushing, or being tentative.

It improves technique and power. Tennis is becoming more of a strength-related sport. Most of the top players are great athletes, and unless players develop their athletic ability to its maximum potential, they cannot compete at the higher levels of the game.

It reduces the number and severity of injuries. This is the most important reason for following a physical training program. The tennis circuit is so strenuous now, even on the collegiate and junior levels, that the tennis player's body must withstand more strain from competition than ever before. A thorough program of physical training will reduce injuries, if not eliminate them. The training program must include flexibility, strength training and a good running program.

It delays fatigue in competition. The development of muscular endurance through physical training enables an athlete to participate at a higher intensity for longer periods of time, thereby enhancing performance later in the competition.

It promotes quick recovery after competition. Muscular endurance developed through a good physical training program enables an athlete to compete day after day at a consistent level of excellence. Most athletes can compete very well early in a tournament, but by the fourth or fifth day their bodies tend to break down under physical stress. A well-conditioned athlete can go many days in a row and recover quickly after each performance.

It reduces the number of "tired hours" after training. High school and college athletes have to study after practice. Even casual players might have important things to do after a match. An athlete in top condition can recover quickly from a workout session or match, no matter how strenuous, and be ready to study or go about the business of the day.

It enables the tennis player to become a better athlete. Athletic ability has become very important in tennis. A strict training program significantly improves strength, flexibility, speed, agility, power, and other motor skills. Through the improvement of these areas, the athlete's overall performance will improve dramatically.

Figure 3-1 shows a schedule of the physical training that a tennis player should undergo in a week. It is essential for a player to follow a good flexibility program every day to relax the body before competition, to guard against the possibility of injury during the match, and to alleviate any soreness from previous performances.

Static (non-moving) stretching exercises should be done, but ballistic stretch exercises or any type of bouncing stretch exercises are not recommended. An anaerobic program of training should be followed three or four days a week, and aerobic training should be included at least one day a week.

CATCHING A SECOND WIND

All tennis players benefit from a running program, because they are more likely to prevail in long, grueling matches.

It is important, however, to incorporate the proper running program into training. Many athletes believe that distance running develops the endurance needed to play a long match, and they run great distances religiously without asking themselves if they are doing the proper thing. They are not.

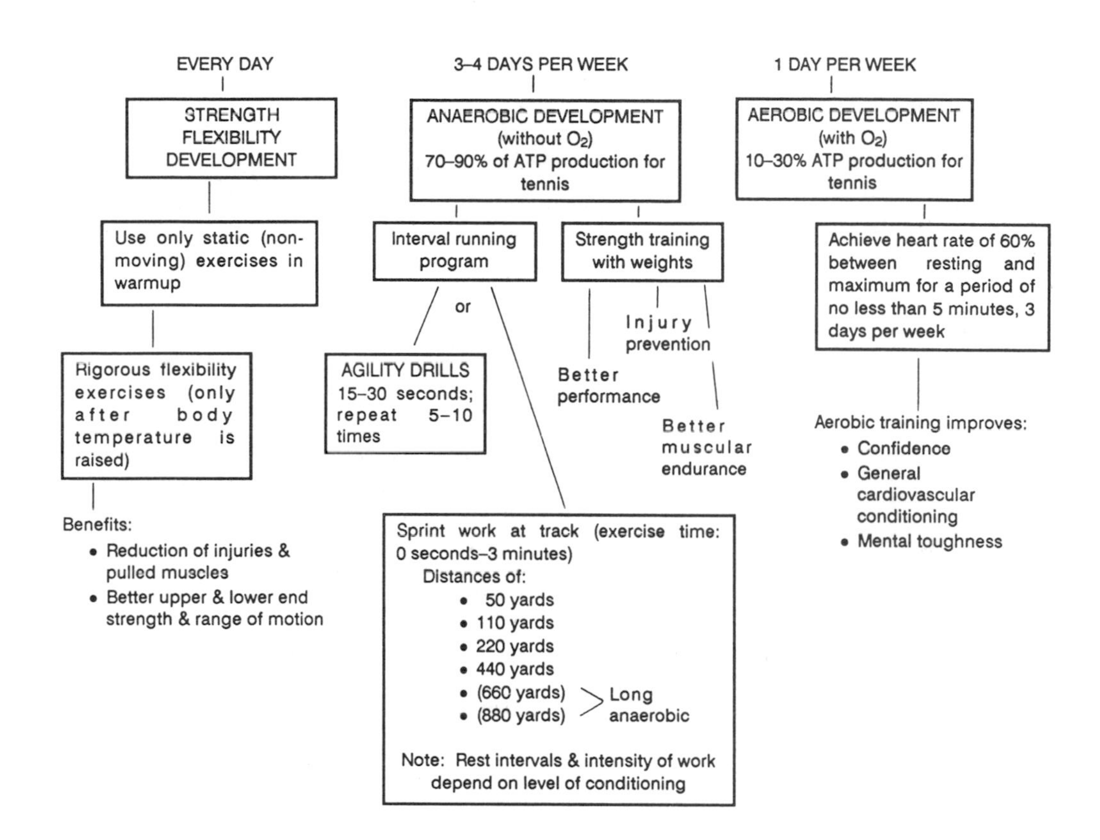

Figure 3-1. Outline of a weekly tennis training program.

Distance running makes use of the aerobic (oxygen) system. Playing tennis makes use of another energy system. A top-level tennis player must be able to replenish his or her anaerobic (without oxygen) system following several high-intensity work periods. This is not the same as being able to withstand a continuous, low-intensity workload over a long period of time, such as when running a long distance.

A tennis player could run five or six miles a day and still be out of shape to play a match, for the same reason a sprinter would not be properly conditioned by running distances instead of running at maximum intensity for shorter amounts of time with rest intervals between each effort.

According to Fox and Matthews' *Interval Training*, 70 to 90 percent of the energy expended by a tennis player must be derived from the anaerobic (without oxygen) system. This means that the body, to produce the energy needed to play tennis, uses the energy stored in the muscles. The chemical names of these energy sources are adenosine triphosphate (ATP) and phosphocreatine (PC), as well as glucose, which is broken down to lactic acid.

Each point in tennis is an all-out explosive type of exercise. Therefore, to gain maximum results, training sessions should simulate the playing of a point. Distance running, however, may be used for losing weight, for breaking the monotony of a training routine, or for general cardiovascular exercise.

Interval Training

The concept of interval training is to train at the most efficient intensity for short periods, rest to enable the lactic acid level to subside, and then resume the workout at the previous level of intensity. Figures 3-2 and 3-3 show why this is more efficient than conventional training without rest periods.

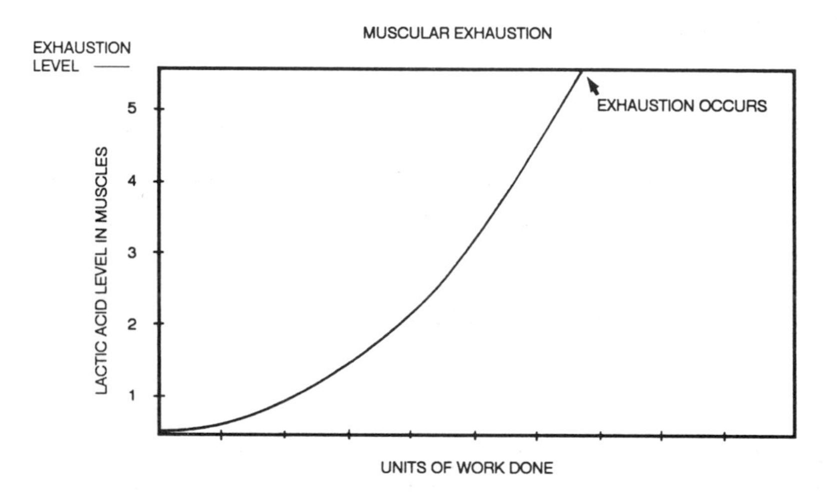

Figure 3-2. Conventional non-interval training

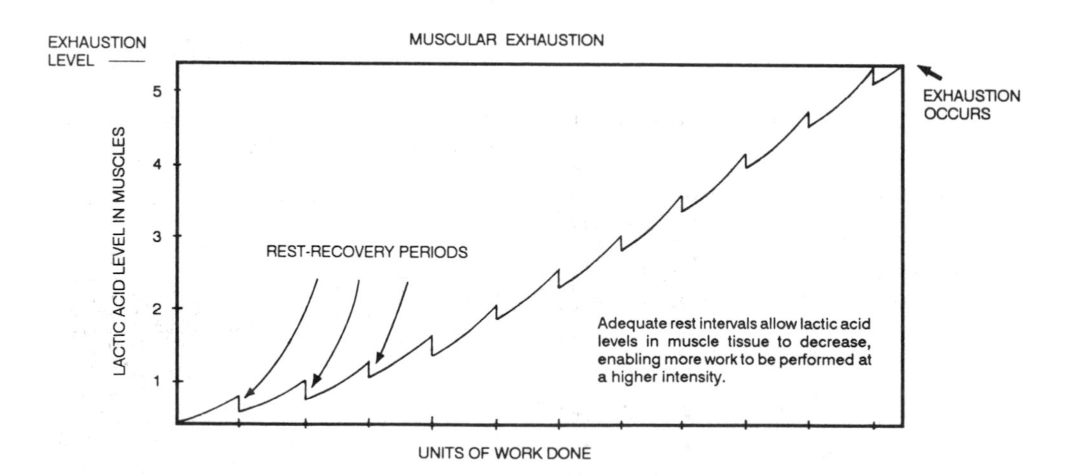

Figure 3-3. Interval training

The amount of work that can be done by muscle tissue depends greatly on lactic acid levels within that tissue. If the level is kept down with intermittent periods of rest, the muscle can perform more work at greater intensity (see figure 3-3). Without adequate rest periods, the lactic acid levels soar, thus paralyzing the muscle and limiting efficiency of performance (see figure 3-2).

As training progresses, an athlete can exercise for longer and longer periods, with reduced rest periods between.

Exercise periods must be at least as intense as the competition for which the athlete is training, or the training effect will not be adequate. Anaerobic interval training, therefore, is recommended over aerobic training for the tennis player. High intensity sessions with adequate rest intervals are the key.

Running drills

1. Sprint 50 yards 8-10 times with rest between each sprint.
2. Sprint 100 yards 6-8 times with 2-2½ minutes rest between each sprint.
3. Sprint 220 yards 4-5 times with 3-4 minutes rest between each sprint.
4. Sprint 440 yards 2-3 times with 5-7 minutes rest between each sprint.

Note: The longer sprints should be done early in the training period and the shorter, more intense sprints after the athlete has a good base.

Agility drills

Service box drill. Start in the center of the service box, facing the net. Shuffle as quickly as possible from one side to the other, touching the center service line and the singles sideline with your foot, using a cross-over step and bending the back knee low to the ground to simulate volley footwork. The hands should be in the volley position. You can also run forward, backward or at an angle. Do this drill for 20 seconds at maximum rate and repeat up to five times, resting for approximately one minute between each execution.

Alley touch drill. For quicker feet, do the same drill as above, but use the 4½-foot alley instead. Again, use footwork that simulates the volley.

Service box drill *Alley touch drill.*

Suicide line touch drill. Start at the doubles sideline and sprint first to the singles sideline and back, then to the center service line and back, then to the opposite singles sideline and back, and finally to the opposite doubles sideline and back to the starting position. Do this drill up to five times with approximately 30 seconds rest between each execution.

Ball drill. Two people are needed for this drill. Your partner kneels down with two balls and rolls them, one at a time, to your right side and then to your left side. You must retrieve the balls one at a time and toss them back, always remembering to face your partner and use good tennis footwork. Use the same hand in which you hold your racquet to pick up every ball so that you will be forced to put your body weight forward on the correct foot as if you were playing a shot.

Suicide line drill. *Ball drill.*

Jumping exercises

Bench blasts. Place one foot on a bench (or chair) and keep the other on the ground. Push off as hard as possible with the leg on the bench, come back down, and then immediately push off again. Repeat 20 to 25 times on each leg for one set. Do three sets of exercises on each leg and rest for one minute between each set. Use a bench high enough to give good resistance but not so high as to put undue strain on the knee joint. If knee strain or lower back strain results from this exercise, it should be discontinued. This is a strenuous exercise and should be performed only by the most well-trained athletes.

Australian double-knee jump. Jump high enough into the air to touch the knees to the chest and then return to the ground. This should be done at maximum intensity 20 to 30 times for a set. Complete up to three sets with a 30 to 45 second rest between each.

Bench blasts. *Australian double-knee jump.*

Power jumping. A weighted jump rope is an excellent way to build anaerobic endurance, muscular endurance, and strength. A good workload is five sets of 50 seconds with at least 75 revolutions per set, resting 50 seconds between each set.

Speed rope jumping. A speed rope and a weighted jump rope complement each other very well. In the training routine, the speed rope should be used for just that — speed. High intensity single or double jumps for periods of 30 to 45 seconds are excellent, and up to five sets should be done with equal rest intervals between sets.

STRENGTH AND FLEXIBILITY

For years, many people have believed that strength training is not good for tennis players' development, believing it makes them clumsy and hamper their flexibility. Actually, strength improvement is one of the best ways to enhance your game. It has been shown that muscular strength is important for the following reasons:

- It reduces the number and severity of injuries and delays fatigue.
- It decreases recovery time from training stress, thereby reducing the number of "tired hours" after training, making it possible to have more consecutive days of good physical performance.
- It increases confidence, because it enhances better technique, stroke production, power, and speed of movement.

Flexibility is the range of motion of any joint in the body. The greater the range of motion, the greater the flexibility. Flexibility is a crucial conditioning component, particularly for advanced players. Contrary to some beliefs, athletes can have both strength and flexibility — a gymnast, for example, has the strength of a linebacker and the flexibility of a dancer. Strong muscles will not hamper flexibility if they are developed through exercises employing a wide range of motion.

A tennis fitness program should combine strength training and flexibility exercises. For ultimate benefits, strength work should be performed three days each week, with the days between devoted to a good running program. Time should be devoted to balance, agility and stretching each day. Figure 3-4 shows a sample strength training and flexibility program.

MON.	TUES.	WED.	THURS.	FRI.	SAT.	SUN.
- Anaerobic exercises - Endurance work - Speed work	- Strength-flexibility training - Optional agility drills	- Anaerobic exercises - Endurance work - Speed work	- Strength-flexibility training - Optional agility drills	- Anaerobic exercises - Endurance work - Speed work	- Strength-flexibility training	- One-day rest or light aerobic workout

Figure 3-4. Flexibility strength training program.

If you are playing tennis as a seasonal sport, the most intense conditioning periods should be in the off-season and the preseason. The program should be tapered after the season starts, but never should be abandoned. After a base of fitness is established in the preseason, it can be maintained with well-timed and well-planned workouts. Optimally, players should focus heavily on physical training before the season or early in the playing period, and taper their workouts as the season or schedule progresses.

Equipment

Nautilus equipment increases the range of motion of each joint and stretches the muscle when exercised. When using free weights or a universal gym, pay special attention to the range of motion and the specificity of each exercise to maintain, and perhaps increase, flexibility.

Determining the proper weight load is critical for strength development. Too little weight does not produce quality results, but too much weight can cause poor technique or even injury. (The same principle relates to racquet weight. If your racquet is too heavy or too light, you may have difficulty executing proper strokes.)

Usually, eight to 12 lift repetitions work well. Try to follow the interval training guidelines from the chapter on Anaerobic Endurance as they relate to muscular work and energy expenditure.

Exercises

If a player does not have access to a weight training facility, the following exercises can be used to increase flexibility and strength. Notice that many of them have been adapted to increase the range of motion.

Keep in mind that quality is much more important than quantity. For example, it is better to do six to 10 repetitions at maximum intensity than to do 30 consecutive repetitions at a lower intensity. The preferred exercise load is two or three sets of 10 repetitions with a rest period of between 30 to 60 seconds between sets, and three to four workouts per week.

Pectoral (chest) exercises

Men's chair-aided push-up

Strokes aided: High forehand and forehand volley.

Description: Unlike conventional push-ups on the ground that only allow half of the full range of motion, performing this exercise on three chairs not only places greater demand on the muscles, it permits a more complete range of motion for the pectoral muscles and triceps. Place your feet on one chair and a hand on each of the other two chairs. Do regular push-ups, making sure to lower your chest as low as possible between the two chairs.

Women's deep chair aided push-up

Strokes aided: Forehand volley and high forehand.

Description: Use the same method described in the men's version, except keep the feet on the ground instead of using a third chair.

Men's deep chair aided push-up.

Women's deep chair aided push-up.

Posterior deltoid and shoulder exercises

Supine lateral raise

Strokes aided: Backhand and backhand volley.

Description: Lie on a bench or couch on your side so that your right arm comes across your chest and hangs freely to the floor. Hold a small dumbbell or weight in your right hand and elevate it in a backhand motion, using only the shoulder. Repeat on the left side.

Chair dip

Strokes aided: This exercise aids in the development of the triceps for serving and promotes good shoulder strength for all strokes, especially high ground strokes, volleys, and out-of-position shots. It is often used by pole vaulters to develop tricep strength.

Description: Place both hands behind your back and on one chair and place your feet on another chair. Using only the elbow joint, lower your body and then raise it back to the starting position.

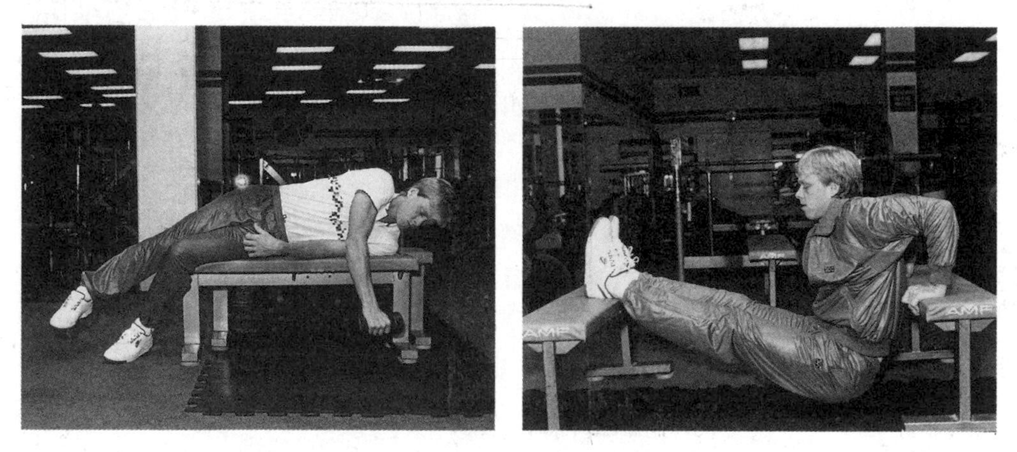

Supine lateral raise. *Chair dip.*

Tricep exercises

Tricep press or French curl

Strokes aided: Service and overhead smash. This exercise improves your serving power dramatically in one to two months. The tricep is the primary muscle used for the service motion. Its contraction straightens out the arm. The three joints used in serving are the shoulder, the elbow, and the wrist.

Description: Stand and hold a dumbbell or hand weight in your right hand and point your elbow up toward the ceiling (it may be supported by the opposite arm). Using only your tricep, straighten your arm out and up. Repeat using the opposite arm.

Tricep press. Wrist curl.

Wrist exercises

Wrist strength is most important for playing the net. The easiest way to exercise the wrists is to use a tennis racquet with a weighted head. The suggested exercise load is one to two sets of 10 to 12 repetitions, with adequate rest periods in between.

Wrist curl (flexors)

Strokes aided: All strokes.

Description: With the palm of the hand facing up, use the wrist only to elevate the racquet and weight to a fully flexed position and then lower it. Strength gain will occur in the forearm.

Wrist extension (extensors)

Strokes aided: All strokes.

Description: With the palm of the hand facing down, use the wrist only to elevate the racquet and then lower it. The back of the forearm is developed.

Neutral position curl

Strokes aided: All strokes.

Description: With the racquet held in an eastern forehand grip (racquet head perpendicular to the ground), elevate the weight using only the wrist. This helps to keep the racquet up on volleys.

Wrist pronation and supination

Strokes aided: All strokes.

Description: With the racquet head pointed straight up, use the wrist to twist the racquet to the left and then to the right. This will strengthen your pronator and supinator muscles for added help in hitting top spin on both sides.

Abdominal exercises

The abdominal muscles should receive special attention, because the power for strokes and overall athletic performance originates in the stomach. The hyperextension exercises of the abdominal area not only significantly increase the strength of that area, but also increase flexibility of the abdominal muscles for prevention of injuries.

Sit-ups, stomach crunches and other abdominal exercises should be done regularly for general conditioning if equipment is not available. The suggested exercise load for abdominal exercises is eight to 15 repetitions in two to three sets.

Note: If a Roman bench is not available, the following exercises can be done on a regular bench or table, or with the use of a partner to hold the legs in position.

Roman bench sit-up

Strokes aided: Overhead smash, serve.

Description: Sit at the edge of a Roman bench and lean down as far as possible to extend the abdominal muscles to the point of slight discomfort. Then proceed to do sit-ups. This exercise should only be done by serious athletes who are in excellent condition; the "everyday player" should stick with traditional sit-ups.

Roman bench back raise

Strokes aided: Overhead smash, serve.

Description: Use either a Roman bench or have a partner restrain your legs. Lie face down with your lower abdominal area touching the edge of the bench. Go from a flexed position to a fully extended position, arching your back upward.

Roman bench external oblique exercise

Stroke aided: Serve.

Description: Lie on your side on a Roman bench with your upper body off the bench and cross your legs so that firm support can be given by a partner who holds your feet. Lower your upper body to the ground as far as possible until slight discomfort is felt in your side abdominal muscles and then return to the starting position.

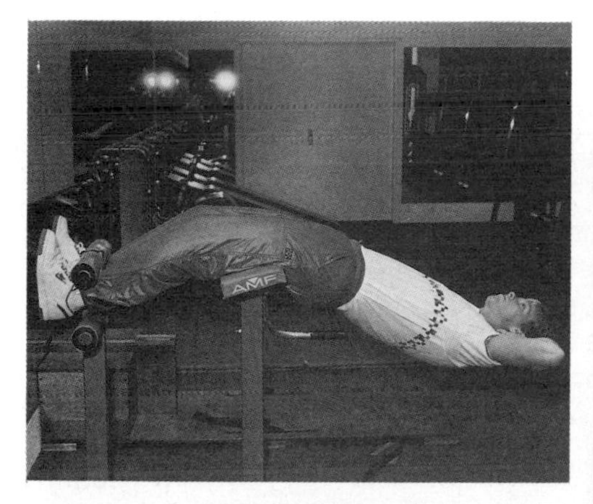

Roman bench sit-up

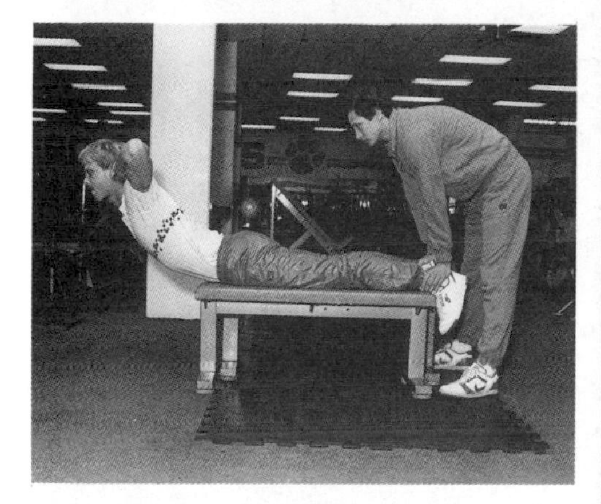

Roman bench back raise.

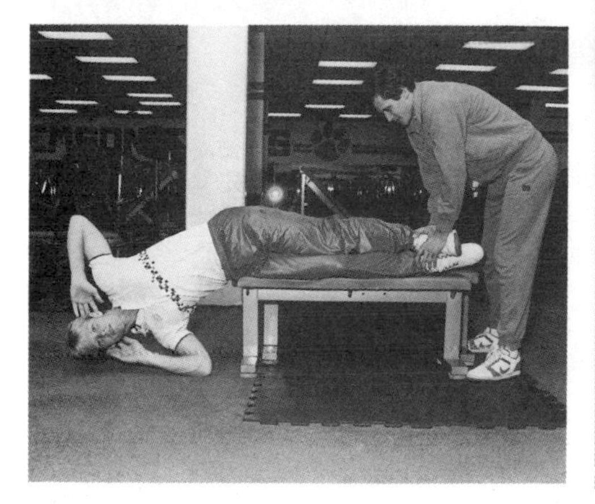

Roman bench external oblique.

Development of the abdominal muscles is important, because they power the serve's coiling action.

Flexibility Training

All athletes should stretch before and after each practice session and match. Many people neglect stretching afterward, but doing so aids in the removal of lactic acid from the muscles, which helps decrease recovery time.

In static stretching exercises, a joint is held for 15 to 30 seconds in a position that stretches the tissue to its maximum controllable length without undue stress. Static (non-moving) stretching is safer than ballistic (balancing or oscillating) methods because it does not impose sudden stress upon the involved tissue, yet does the work intended. Proper stretching also aids in relieving tension from daily stress.

The following guidelines should be observed when stretching:

- Never force a stretching muscle during the exercise to a level of discomfort or pain. Do not overstretch.
- Be patient; work within your limits.
- Stay relaxed in all areas of the body.
- Maintain good posture and body alignment at all times.
- Do not hold your breath — breathe normally.
- Always do some sort of aerobic warm-up exercises before stretching.
- Use equal time intervals between exercises to let the muscles relax (10 to 30 seconds).

The following are common stretching exercises:

Calf stretch.

Standing shin stretch.

Calf stretch

Muscles stretched: Calf, lower hamstrings.

Description: Stand erect with your feet together and both heels on the ground. Lean forward against a wall or immovable object. Then lean farther until tightness is felt in the calves and Achilles tendons. Hold this position for 30 seconds and then return to the original position.

Standing shin stretch

Muscles stretched: Tibialis anterior, shin and ankle muscles.

Description: Stand erect with your back to a wall and your feet flat on the ground. Lean backward until tightness is felt in the shin muscles. Turn the toes outward, and then inward for different angles. (This may be done with one leg or both legs at a time.) Hold each position for 30 seconds and then return to the starting position.

Sitting shoulder stretch. *Scissor back stretch.*

Sitting shoulder stretch

Muscles stretched: Shoulder and neck muscles.

Description: Sit down with the legs together pointing forward. Your arms are behind your body, with your palms on the floor and your fingers pointing toward your body. Slowly lean back and increase the angle between your arms and your trunk until maximum stretch is achieved. Hold this position for 30 seconds and return to the original position.

Scissor back stretch

Muscles stretched: Lower back muscles, buttocks, upper hamstrings.

Description: Lie on your back with your legs together and your arms extended out at the sides. Slowly raise the right leg to reach the left arm. Hold this position for 30 seconds. Return to the original position and repeat, this time raising the left leg to reach the right arm.

Standing hamstring stretch.

Standing shoulder stretch.

Standing hamstring stretch

Muscles stretched: Hamstring, lower back muscles, upper calf muscle.

Description: Stand upright with the knees locked. Bend forward slowly, moving the hands toward the ankles until tightness is felt in the hamstrings. Hold this position for 30 seconds, and then slowly return to the original position.

Standing shoulder stretch

Muscles stretched: Front and back shoulder and neck muscles.

Description: Stand with your arms straight out to your sides and hold a stationary object. Turn slowly to the left and slowly stretch the shoulder until tightness is felt. Hold this position for 30 seconds. Return to the starting position and repeat, turning to the right.

Pretzel stretch

Muscles stretched: Lower back, buttocks, upper shoulder.

Description: Sit with the right leg bent at the knee with the upper leg flat on the floor. Raise the left knee and place the left foot flat on the floor next to the right knee. Slowly twist the torso to the left. The right arm should be placed outside the raised knee to facilitate twist. Hold for 30 seconds and return to the original position. Repeat the procedure on the opposite side.

Static groin stretch

Muscles stretched: Groin muscles.

Description: Sit down, and pull your heels together toward the groin. Slowly push down on your knees with your elbows until tightness is felt in the groin area. Hold for 30 seconds and return to the original position.

Pretzel stretch.

Static groin stretch.

Hurdler's hamstring stretch

Muscles stretched: Hamstring muscles.

Description: Sit on the floor with one leg turned backward, but not as to put excess strain on the knee joint, and the other extended forward (hurdler's position). Bend the torso down toward the knee until tightness is felt. Hold this position for 30 seconds, and then slowly return to the original position.

Sprinter's stretch

Muscles stretched: Groin area muscles, gastrocnemius (calf), hamstring, quadriceps, upper back muscles.

Description: Stand in an upright position with the knees locked. Slowly spread the legs apart forward and backward as far as you can. Slowly move the hands toward the right ankle until tightness is felt in the hamstring and gastrocnemius, and hold this position for 30 seconds. Return to the original position and repeat for the left leg.

Hurdler's hamstring stretch. *Sprinter's stretch.*

Cobra stretch

Muscles stretched: Abdominal muscles, upper quadriceps.

Description: Lie flat on your stomach. Push your upper body off the floor with hands extending up to full stretch. Hold for 30 seconds. Slowly return to the original position.

Hurdler's quadricep stretch

Muscles stretched: Quadriceps, shin muscles.

Description: Lie on your back with your legs together. Point one leg out to the side and the other straight ahead. Lower your head toward the floor until tightness is felt in the quadriceps. Do not put pressure on the knee of the leg extended to the side. Hold this position for 30 seconds. Slowly return to the original position and repeat with the right leg.

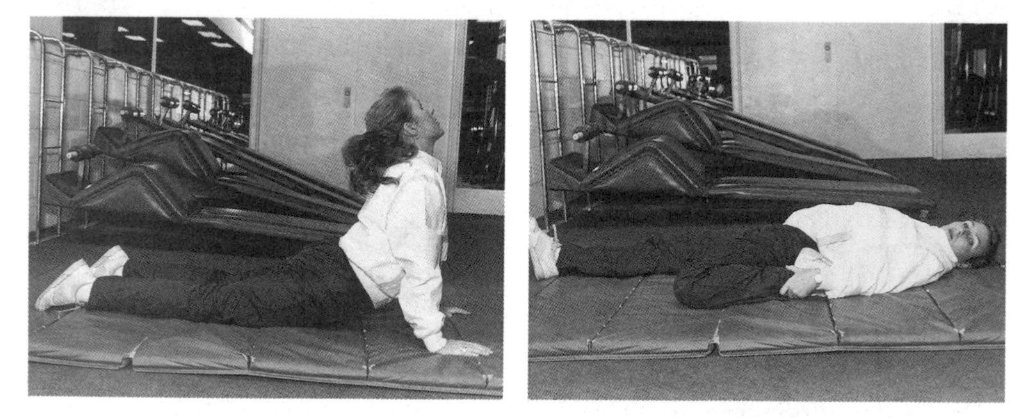

Cobra stretch. *Hurdler's quadricep stretch.*

Exercises for wrist flexors and extensors

The following wrist exercises should be done in a contraction-relaxation manner. The opposite hand should be used as the resisting force to enable the isometric contraction. Extension should be done to the point of muscle tightness and slight resistance. The wrist should then be extended slightly farther and the exercise repeated. Three extensions and contractions should be sufficient for each exercise.

Wrist flexor stretch

Description: The palm of the racquet hand should be facing up. With the opposite hand, pull the racquet hand and fingers downward so that the muscles and connective tissues of the wrist are extended.

Wrist extensor stretch

Description: The palm of the racquet hand should be facing down. With the opposite hand, press the hand and fingers downward, extending the muscles and connective tissues of the wrist.

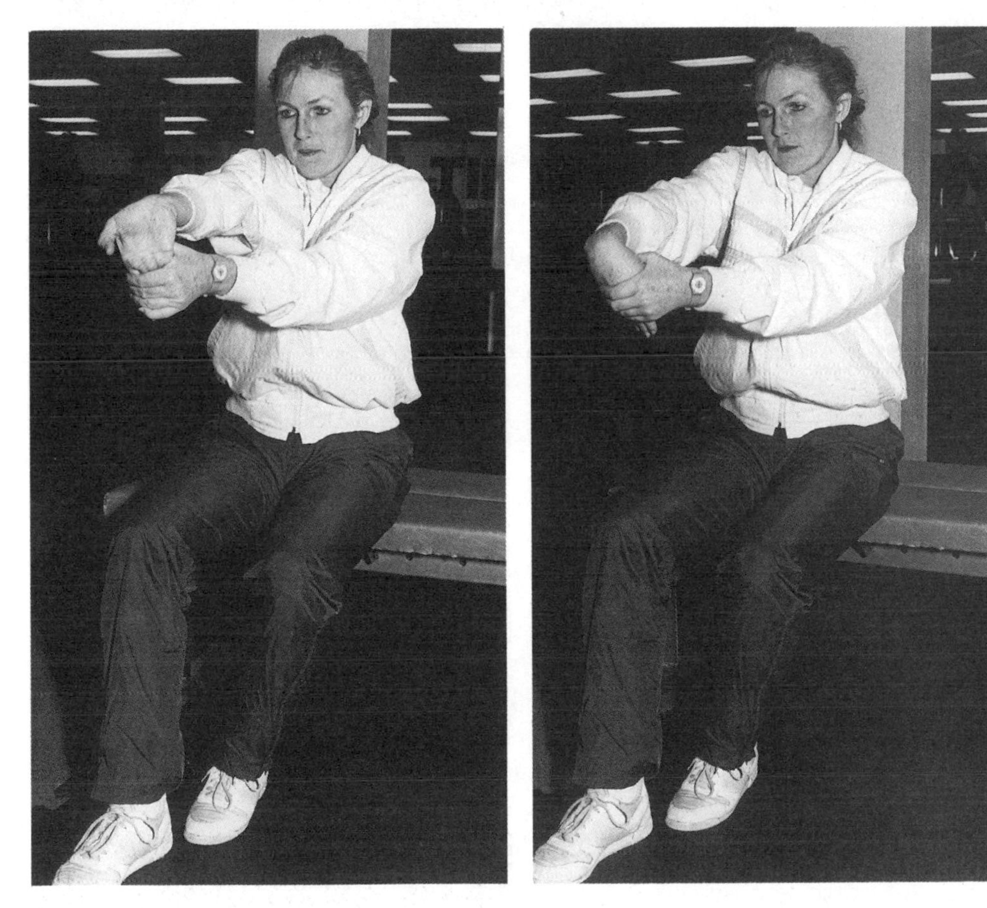

Wrist flexor stretch. *Wrist extensor stretch.*

Neutral position stretch

Description: Hold the racquet in an eastern forehand grip, with the racquet head perpendicular to the ground. Let the racquet head face forward toward the ground, extending the muscles on the top of the wrist. Keeping the racquet head in a neutral position, add slight pressure for a very gradual stretch.

Tricep and service stretch

Description: Hold the racquet behind your back. The racquet should be dropped straight down your back as a slow gradual stretch is done.

Neutral position stretch. *Tricep and service stretch.*

Pronation muscle stretch

Description: Hold a racquet with the racquet head pointing straight up (12 o'clock position) and then rotate it clockwise to a 3 o'clock or 4 o'clock position. At this extended position, the opposite hand is used as the resister and the contract-relaxation exercise is done. The racquet is then rotated farther to a 4:30 or 5 o'clock position, and the exercise is repeated.

Supination muscle stretch

Description: Hold a racquet with the racquet head pointing straight up (12 o'clock) and then rotate it counterclockwise to an 8 o'clock or 9 o'clock position. Provide resistance with the opposite hand and do contract-relaxation exercises. The racquet is then rotated farther to a 7 o'clock or 7:30 position and the exercise is repeated.

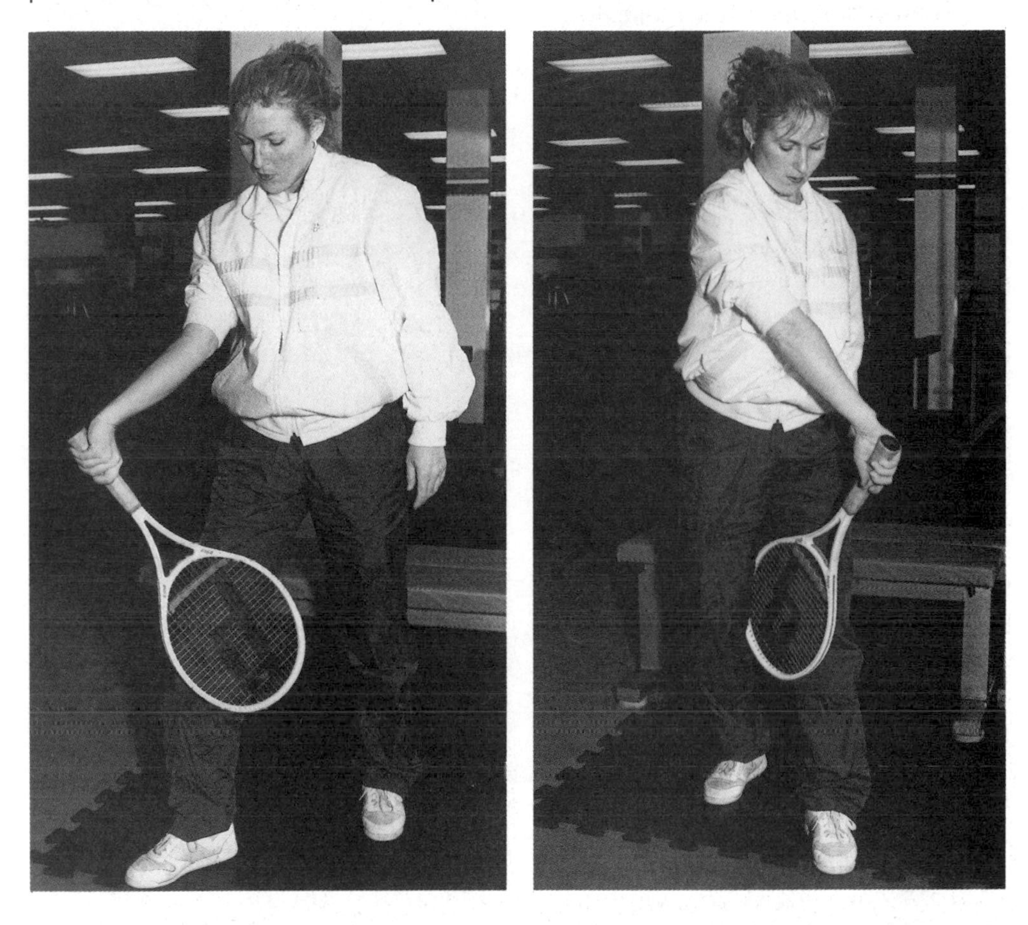

Pronation muscle stretch. *Supination muscle stretch.*

REVVING THE MOTOR SKILLS

Tennis is a complex sport, in part because of the many different motor skills that are involved. Speed, agility, balance, reaction time, quickness, power, and hand-eye coordination are all important. Athletes do not have enough time in practice to work on each of these areas, so most coaches try to incorporate a training program that encompasses many of them. The primary areas of importance to tennis are speed, agility, and balance.

Speed in tennis usually refers to a player's foot movement, or how quickly a player can move from point A to point B on the court. A player that can run down balls that are out of reach for the average player has a tremendous advantage. Bjorn Borg summed it up nicely when he said, "A tennis match is the running of 1,000 10-yard dashes."

Many other motor skills are involved, though. Each time a tennis player hits a ball, reaction time, quickness, and power are important factors. Reaction time, or "the time between the stimulus and the initial response," becomes a key ingredient in any quick exchange of shots. Quickness refers to an athlete's short spurts of speed. Power is the combination of speed and strength. Power often is categorized as the greatest component of athletic ability, but in tennis the saying "power thrills, but speed kills" is very true. Both power and speed should be trained for best results on the court.

Agility is "the physical ability that enables an individual to rapidly change positions and direction in a precise manner." In tennis, the need for this motor skill is quite obvious, because all stroke production is based on the ability to get from one area of the court to another, to set up, to remain balanced and to change direction.

Speed agility refers to a player's ability to move quickly while remaining in perfect balance so that a quick stop and change of direction can be made. Without the ability to get to the ball and then set up for a good stroke, good technical skills are useless. Lack of this combination of speed and agility can prevent a player from progressing to a higher level of performance.

When a player starts falling behind in a match, a common complaint is, "I can't feel the ball," or "I don't know why I'm missing the ball." This is another way of saying the player is having difficulty setting up for shots, and the shots are not effective. The player is lacking speed and balance.

Professional players' careers falter after they lose their speed and balance, because they can no longer make effective shots. In fact, speed is always the first thing to go as a player ages or fails to train properly. Again, it should be emphasized that speed alone is not lost; it is the loss of speed, agility, and balance, the three key ingredients to effective stroke production. Without them, it does not matter what the body is doing from the waist up.

Balance, or the ability to hold a stationary position, is also a very important element of a tennis player's athletic ability. Solid and well-placed shots cannot be made without this important motor skill. The researcher Bass believes the ability to balance easily might depend on the functions of the mechanisms in the semicircular canals; the kinesthetic sensations in the muscles, tendons, and joints; the visual perception while the body is in motion; and the ability to coordinate these three sources of stimuli. Balance is very much an inherited skill, but it can be improved through proper training.

All running and agility drills should emphasize good balance, as should stroking work. The reminder "head down and feet on the ground" is critical to the development of balance in stroke production. Good balance enables a player's technical skills to remain effective longer and enables maximum leverage for power and accuracy even if the athlete is not strong.

The following sample 45-minute training routine helps develop motor skills. All drills should simulate the speed, agility, and balance used in match play. The footwork, when possible, should simulate the footwork used when executing a stroke. (Participants should warm up properly first.)

1. Five minutes: Jog and stretch

2. Five minutes: Jump rope, alternating the weighted rope with the speed rope (five times, 30-second intervals with 30-second rest periods)

3. Ten minutes:

    a. Box drills: two sets (30 seconds rest).

    b. Bench blasts: two sets each leg (30 seconds rest).

    c. Alley quick step drills: two sets (30 seconds rest).

    d. 30-yard sprints: six sets (10 seconds rest).

4. Five minutes: Foot control ball drills (dribble a tennis ball alternating feet in order to improve balance and control).

5. Two minutes: Jump rope, cool down.

6. Five minutes: Rest break.

7. Two minutes: Warm up with a jump rope.

8. Five minutes: Lateral court movement drills, ball pickup drills, lateral movement.

9. Three minutes: Power jump rope, alternate 45 seconds exercise, 15 seconds rest.

10. Two minutes: Bench blast.

11. Two minutes: Jump rope, cool down.

Training for motor skills.

It also is important to understand the relationship between fast twitch and slow twitch muscle tissues. The body's striated (skeletal) muscles contain two types of fibers: dark fibers (slow twitch) and light fibers (fast twitch). Dark muscle fibers have slow contractions but great endurance, whereas light muscle fibers have quick contractions but little endurance.

This relationship is easily understood by looking at a chicken or a quail. Both of these birds have light muscle fibers in the breast and dark muscle fibers in the legs. Neither can fly far, but each has strong legs. A duck's breast has only dark muscle fibers that aid the long, slow flight to Canada and back.

This relationship can be seen in fish as well. The dark muscle tissue of salmon and trout gives them the endurance they need to travel great distances upstream to spawn. Bass and bream have light muscle tissue that enables quick bursts of speed, but both of these fish fatigue easily.

Dark and light muscle fibers are interspersed throughout all human muscles. It may be true that sprinters have a higher proportion of light muscle fibers, whereas distance runners have a higher proportion of dark fibers. Tennis players, however, must train both types of muscle tissue.

Tennis is predominantly an anaerobic sport that requires high intensity and ballistic speed, so training should be geared toward the fast muscles. Exercises such as bench blasts, double-knee jumps, sprints, suicide line drills, and speed jump rope work are all excellent for this. Training of the slow twitch muscles also is important to help prevent injuries, for joint and connective tissue strength, and for muscular endurance. Excellent slow twitch work can be done with Nautilus equipment, other weight programs, or exercises designed to improve strength and speed.

EATING RIGHT

An athlete may have the best training program in the world, but the effort will be wasted unless sound nutrition practices also are followed. Young tennis players may believe they do not need to worry about their diets, but this is not true. Proper diet can influence performance, and sometimes makes the difference between winning and losing.

For example, a few years back we had been training for six weeks in preparation for our first major tournament at the University of Miami. My players were in top shape mentally and physically. I was particularly concerned about the heat and humidity in southern Florida, so the week before the tournament I had each player take a steam bath for 10 to 15 minutes every day and wear nylon rainsuits during their workouts to make them perspire more than they normally did during workouts.

I thought I had covered everything, but I had forgotten one important detail — I had not monitored the eating habits of my team.

We were playing the University of California-Irvine in a morning match. Halfway through the second set, one of my returning All-Americans was playing very poorly and appeared sluggish. I walked to his court and asked him what was the matter. He said he did not know, except that he could not focus on what he was doing. At first I was upset with him, and gave him a stern pep talk.

As he played another game, I saw a determined but exhausted expression on his face. I knew he was trying hard to concentrate, but something was wrong. He had his head between his legs and looked totally exhausted. I wondered if my training program had been lacking, or if he had been out on the town the night before.

Then a thought struck me. I walked over to him and asked him what he had eaten for breakfast. He replied, "Pancakes with syrup, a Danish, and a glass of orange juice." Then I realized what was happening: he was experiencing a sugar crash from all the sugar he had eaten that morning. For that player, six weeks of training had been wasted because of an order of pancakes and Danish. We lost the match over a very simple detail that I should have monitored.

Basic Nutritional Guidelines

A proper diet is essential to athletic performance, but many athletes give little or no thought to their dietary needs. Athletes at all levels should know and follow sound nutritional guidelines.

Food is composed of seven basic substances: carbohydrates, fats, proteins, vitamins, minerals, water, or indigestible materials. Each one of these has specific functions in providing nourishment for the body. Athletes should know how each of them affects performance.

Carbohydrates. Complex carbohydrates are metabolized very easily into glucose (blood sugar) to be used for quick energy. Carbohydrates enable the athlete to feel alert, strong, and energetic, and they help to maintain proper blood sugar levels.

Carbohydrates provide four calories of energy per gram. The best sources of carbohydrates are fruit, vegetables, pastas, breads, and cereal products. Carbohydrates are used up very quickly in the athlete's body and should be replaced often. Sugar, though, is a simple carbohydrate and can be harmful. Too much sugar intake can cause lightheadedness, fatigue, and concentration lapse.

Fats. At nine calories per gram, fats provide a long-term energy source. The body uses fat for energy metabolism after carbohydrate supplies are depleted. Fat also is used for insulation and for padding for the body's organs. Fat is much harder to digest than carbohydrates, and too much fat in the diet can cause health problems. Fats are found in many foods, such as butter, oils, peanuts, and meats.

Proteins. Protein should be an important part of an athlete's diet because it helps tissue grow and repair itself. Proteins are used by the body as an energy source only after carbohydrates and fats are depleted, but protein is very difficult to convert to energy, and therefore should be consumed on days the athlete is not competing, or a few hours after competition. Carbohydrates, though, are best for immediate, after-match consumption.

Protein provides four calories per gram. Meat, fish, poultry, legumes, wheat germ, and bean sprouts are good sources of protein.

Vitamins. Vitamins assist body functions and metabolism. They are necessary for cell activity, and are therefore critical to the proper function of the athlete's body. An inadequate diet does not supply all of the necessary vitamins.

Vitamins A, D, E, and K are fat soluble. They are stored in the fat, and it is not necessary to eat them every day. In fact, excessive quantities of fat soluble vitamins can cause sluggishness or indigestion.

Vitamins B and C are water soluble. They are not stored in the body and must be replaced, and any excess will be removed in the urine. A lack of B-complex vitamins in the body may cause muscular fatigue, cramps, and loss of concentration.

Minerals. As with vitamins, minerals are essential to the proper functioning of the body. They participate in hormone and enzyme production and give structure to the bones and other parts of the body.

Calcium, magnesium, phosphorus, sulfhur, sodium chloride, and potassium are needed in large amounts. Others needed in trace amounts are iron, selenium, manganese, fluoride, copper, molybdenum, zinc, chromium, cobalt, and iodine.

Water. Water is important for every bodily function. In fact, the body of a well-conditioned person consists of about 60 percent water. Water enables the cells to work, is a component of blood, and is an important part of the body's cooling system, lymphatic system, and nervous system.

Almost all foods contain water, but naturally the best way to obtain it is by drinking fluids. Water contains no calories, but it is primarily responsible for all energy metabolism.

A recent study had an athlete train on a treadmill to the point of exhaustion, with no water intake. His endurance was just over one hour. The same athlete then exercised again with two water breaks, during which he was given as much water as he wanted, and he doubled his time on the treadmill. The third time the same athlete was given frequent small amounts of water, and he was able to exercise up to four times as long as his original time.

The lesson for the tennis player is to drink water early in the day of competition, and then frequently from the start to the finish of the match, before thirst occurs. It also is important to drink plenty of water the night before a match — 16 to 32 ounces is recommended.

Indigestible materials — fiber and roughage. Cancer of the colon is now the second most common type of cancer in America. Many doctors and nutritionists blame high meat and fat diets, preservatives that are added in so many foods, and diets lacking in foods rich in fiber.

Harmful foods

Sugar. The harmful effects of refined sugars are far-reaching. Two hundred years ago, the average American ate about four pounds of sugar per year. Today, Americans eat an average of 129 pounds of it, or about 2½ pounds per week. Sugar is added to many processed foods, and consumers should be sure to read the ingredient panel on packages of food.

Sugar can cause a condition called reactive hypoglycemia, in which the blood sugar level rises quickly, giving a high feeling of energy. Very quickly the body's balancing system reacts by sending insulin into the bloodstream, which produces a crashing effect that causes depression and reduced concentration. Appetite is controlled by the blood sugar level, and this crash causes great hunger pangs. If these pangs are satisfied by more sugar, an even greater crash is created. Appetite is best controlled by eating complex carbohydrates, such as fruits and vegetables, and eliminating refined sugars.

An athlete who partakes of too much refined sugar will experience many up-and-down swings in moods, concentration, and performance. The best approach is to eat no sugar at all before or during competition.

White flour. White flour lacks many of the important nutrients found in wheat. Whole wheat or other whole grain breads, therefore, are more nutritious than white bread.

Salt tablets. Sodium, magnesium, and potassium are the minerals that are lost through exercise. They are replaced well by fruits and vegetables and fruit juices. The average American consumes far too much salt, and the ingestion of salt tablets can lead to serious dehydration, possible heat exhaustion, and stroke.

Alcohol and beer. Alcohol has a long-lasting effect on athletic performance. One can of beer can lower some athletes' heat tolerance for 24 to 48 hours, and three or more drinks can reduce heat tolerance for days. Lack of coordination may persist until 24 hours after alcohol consumption.

Juice supplements. There has been much discussion about what is the best drink before and during competition. Juice supplements contain varying amounts of potassium, but less than whole milk or orange juice. Milk should not be consumed immediately before or after competition. Perhaps the best drink is a mixture of three parts water and one part fruit juice.

The pregame meal

The old idea of eating a steak and potato before competition is no longer considered a good one. Protein takes a long time to digest, and meat can sometimes sit in the stomach for hours before entering the digestive tract. Carbohydrates, including pasta, breads, fruits, vegetables, and plenty of liquids, are the best pre-game meal. Fats are also hard to digest, but are important for an endurance event. Dairy products should not be ingested before competition, because the calcium may interfere with the magnesium uptake that is important in energy expenditure.

The post-game meal

Athletes are often so hungry after a competition that they run out and grab whatever food they can find. More often than not, they choose sugar-filled foods.

This is harmful, because sugar interferes with the body's metabolism and regulating system. The following day, the athlete may feel sluggish, disoriented, and emotionally sensitive.

The athlete should ingest about 300 calories or 80 to 90 grams of carbohydrates within 30 minutes after a workout. Two bananas with water or another type of fruit would be excellent.

Some coaches closely monitor the diets of their players. They make sure to have juices, fruit, bread, and peanut butter sandwiches in the locker room immediately after a game or match to help take the edge off the players' appetites so they do not go out and load up on sugary foods.

DEALING WITH INJURIES

Tennis players are as active as any other athlete. Although they are not as likely to receive bruises and contusions as athletes in contact sports, the continuous periods of competition cause many stress- and strain-related injuries. The body's connective tissues, such as the tendons and ligaments, are severely tested, and muscle tissue, bursa, tendon sheaths, and other lubricating substances of the body also are at risk.

Tennis has become a year-round sport. Most other sports have an off-season when athletes are able to completely rest and heal, but the constant chase of the next tournament or ranking often forces tennis players back into competition before they are 100 percent. This increases the possibility of reinjury and a further setback.

All tennis players, including recreational participants, and coaches, should understand injury prevention, management, and treatment.

Injury Prevention

Injuries result in loss of training time, so it is very important that tennis players do everything possible to prevent them. The following measures should be part of a tennis player's daily ritual:

Raise the body temperature before practice. The athlete's muscle fibers and connective tissues can be compared to a rubber band. If a rubber band is cold and is jerked quickly in a ballistic manner, it might tear or break. If, however, the same rubber band is warmed and is then very slowly stretched without rapid and jerky moves, it is elastic.

Likewise, a cold muscle that is put through rapid flexing and stretching also might tear. Raising the temperature of the muscle and then slowly stretching it with nonmovement (static) stretching enables effective flexions and extensions. When the body temperature is raised, the speed of contraction and relaxation of the muscles is increased. Light jogging, rope jumping, or calisthenics work well to raise the body temperature.

Use a consistent stretching routine. Stretching enables the muscles to relax and permits the flow of blood and oxygen. Flexibility exercises also help reduce muscle soreness by transport of lactic acid out of fatigued tissues.

However, overstretching might damage ligaments and joints. Therefore, an athlete should follow a familiar program every day that includes solid static (nonmoving) fundamentals.

The following guidelines should be followed in a stretching routine:

- Warm up the body by one degree or until a sweat breaks.
- Use only static (stationary) and gradual exercises. Never use ballistic (moving or bouncing) exercises.
- Stretch all muscle groups.
- Do not overstretch, do not understretch.
- Bring the body to a sweat once more before starting the workout.

Treatment and Management of Injuries

When an injury does occur, it must be properly treated. Injuries can be divided into three categories based on severity of the injury and recurrence. Athletes and coaches should know the proper treatment for each.

Acute injury

An acute injury is an immediate injury, or an injury that occurs by accident during training. Examples include an ankle sprain, muscle tear or broken bone. The athlete cannot compete with this type of injury.

Treatment: Use ice compression and elevation for the first 24 to 48 hours. Never, never use heat or aspirin for the first 48 to 64 hours! Usually a three- or four-day layoff is required for rest. The athlete should see a physician or sports trainer immediately.

Subacute injury

A subacute injury is an injury that builds up over time and hampers play. The Osgood Slaughter knee condition or an overworked, strained muscle are examples. These injuries cause great frustration, because while the athlete can participate, performance is usually hampered.

Treatment: Warm up slowly. Use ice after workout. Anti-inflamatory medications should be used only by doctor's prescription.

Recurrent injury

A recurrent injury is usually a joint injury such as tennis elbow, rotator cuff, and shoulder bursitis. Recurrent injuries can return unpredictably.

Treatment: Warm up slowly. Use ice after the workout, and aspirin and prescriptions *only* under a doctor's supervision.

Note: Ice constricts blood flow to tissue, therefore reducing swelling of an acute injury. Heat dilates blood vessels and speeds blood flow, and can make an injury more severe. Aspirin tends to thin blood, thereby increasing swelling to an injured muscle or joint. When competing with an injury, the athlete should warm up gradually and use ice massage or compression immediately after competition. *Never* use heat on or aspirin with a new injury!

Rehabilitation

Rest and treatment enable the healing process to take place. As pain subsides, athletes often feel ready for full-scale competition again, but they often come back too soon. The major concern is that the rapid atrophy and degeneration of the muscle tissue that takes place leaves athletes extremely susceptible to reinjury. When reinjury occurs, the entire rest and treatment process must take place all over again. This can start a cycle that can be extremely frustrating for competitive athletes.

As pain from an injury starts to subside, athletes should work themselves back into their practice routine gradually. Most of the heavy exercise should be done with the stabilizer or support muscles close to the injury, with activity that does not aggravate the ailment. As the injured area becomes stronger, more and more exercises should be done to make the muscle tissue strong and to prevent reinjury. Taping to restrict movement of the affected area can also be of great help during this rehabilitative period.

"The toughest thing about success
is that you've got to keep on being a success.
Talent is only a starting point.
You've got to keep on working that talent."

— Irving Berlin

4

Realizing Your Potential

One of the things that troubles me most about the way tennis is taught to young players in America is the unreasonable amount of pressure that is placed on the kids. Too many parents and coaches are searching for the next "child prodigy."

Children usually learn physical skills very easily in the early stages of their lives when there's not much pressure, and before physical growth occurs in the early teen years.

We often see a burnout syndrome in tennis, and other sports. The public has been led to believe that the peak years for young players are in their late teens, and even younger for girls. This is completely false! Players learning the game should understand that while physical skills are learned earliest, it takes time to develop the mental and emotional skills needed. A better timetable would be the ages of 18 to 25 for women and 20 to 30 for men, when the mind and emotions can catch up to the physical development. They all have to come together before a player can become successful.

As proof of this, think back to when you were a kid. You probably were quite good at performing some daring feat, only to become fearful of it later when you were old enough to really think about it. When I was 10, I would do triple-flips off of the high dive, build huge ramps with plywood and a big rock and ride my bike off of them, and hunt for snakes. Today, I wouldn't do any of these things.It's the same in tennis. Young kids who feel no pressure love to play the game. But when they get older and expectations arise and they think too much about it, they can have problems.

Physical development, however, is obviously the most crucial aspect of achieving success in tennis or any other sport. How should players improve their skills? Play sets against better players and hope that some of their skills rub off? Or do drill work, over and over again, simulating the shots and situations that are faced in competition? What about physical conditioning? What about the relatively new area called mental training? What about strategy? Do tennis skills just evolve if the game is played long enough? Does a player have time to wait for them to evolve?

Skill Growth

The following graph illustrates growth for most motor skills. Improvement comes quickly at first, with only a moderate amount of time and effort. As players improve their expectations rise, sometimes unrealistically, and it appears that success is only a matter of working a little harder and longer than the next person. This is true until players reach the 50th or 60th percentile of their potential, then a plateau begins to occur. Players must expect the final stages of improvement to come in small increments, a frustrating reality for both players and coaches.

In the early stages of development, a good system for training must be established. It is the coach's job to help players learn their fundamentals and guide them in the development of the right areas at the right pace.

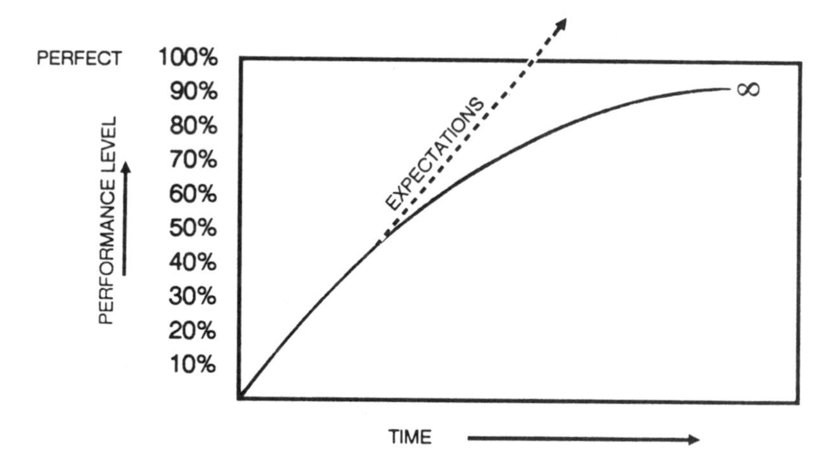

Figure 4-1. The skill growth curve graph.

Hard work is important, but working harder does not always mean working better. When the plateau in the learning curve occurs, hard work alone will not always bring improvement, so the goal of the player should be to work hard *and* to work smart. The athlete must find the ingredient, whether it is physical, mental, or emotional, that brings improvement.

After it is understood that plateaus and barriers do exist, the athlete and coach can plan the next few percentages of improvement. It's exciting to discover that a one-percent improvement for the athlete at a higher level might separate that person from many other players.

The great improvements made by John McEnroe in 1978 and by Boris Becker in 1985 are good examples. Ironically, both players made the jump as a result of excellent performances at Wimbledon, the most prestigious of all tournaments. It's ridiculous to think that such improvement took place entirely in the space of a few days with a few wins at a big tournament. Both players were physically capable of the feat before that tournament, and as they gained momentum from each win, they became more confident.

The next phase of growth, the most critical one, was being comfortable with their new roles and the host of responsibilities that accompanied them. Often players collapse and retreat after advancing to a new level because of a reluctance to accept all that it takes to stay there; often they cannot deal with the new expectations that success brings them.

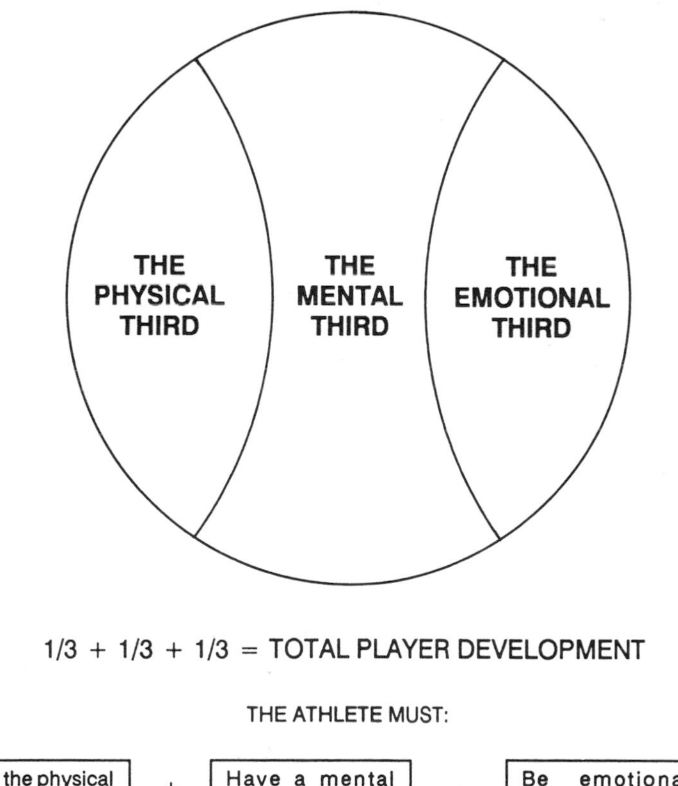

1/3 + 1/3 + 1/3 = TOTAL PLAYER DEVELOPMENT

THE ATHLETE MUST:

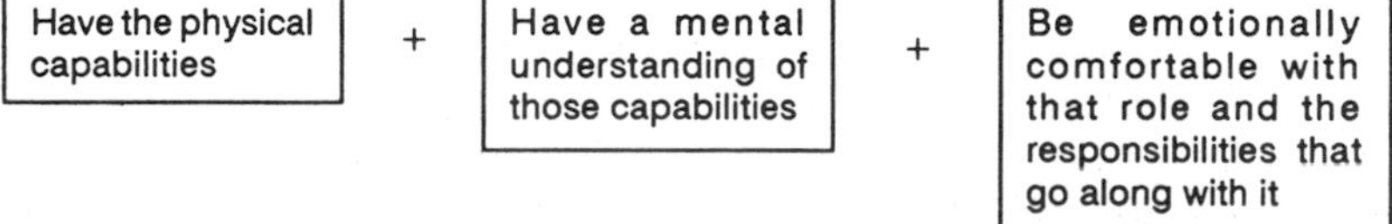

Figure 4-2. Total player development.

Total Player Development

Philosophers, psychologists, and teachers all testify to the three areas of human development: the physical, the mental, and the emotional. Tennis players must also develop as people in order for their games to benefit. Not only must they be physically capable of the necessary skills, they must have confidence in their ability, and, most importantly, be emotionally comfortable with each new level of play and its responsibilities.

In the early stages of development, the physical skills must be emphasized. They are the foundation without which the other areas cannot be developed. Later, the mental aspect is developed, enabling the physical to become functional. The last area to be developed is the emotional, which either enables the mental and the physical to work together, or if it is lacking, becomes the monkey wrench that eventually breaks down the machinery.

Athletes and coaches must be discerning in picking out the area of growth that the athlete most needs. They must recognize that, in the learning stages, development must progress from the physical to the mental and then to the emotional, but that in the functional stage, it must operate in the exact opposite sequence. Quality physical performances are possible only with the understanding that the emotional areas enable the mental areas to function, which in turn, enable the physical areas to engage fully.

Each area has unique components and, for the total development of the athlete, each must be trained. Athletes have a tendency to go through physical motions robotically without engaging the mental and emotional aspects. Too often, the athlete relies on a coach to supply these areas. The athlete must share the responsibility for these areas as well before total development can occur.

"Be not afraid of growing slowly,
be only afraid of standing still."

— Chinese proverb

5

Learning the Strokes

I was fortunate after college to work for Harry Hopman, who was the Australian Davis Cup Coach for more than 20 years. Hopman has been recognized as one of the greatest coaches of all time, and his results with players such as Rod Laver, Ken Rosewall, and Roy Emerson may never be equaled. Having had little formal tennis training at that point, I was expecting to learn all the new techniques and the mechanics of hitting the ball.

In my first month of working for Hopman, I was surprised and somewhat disappointed to find that I was not learning all the fancy schoolbook techniques of the great players that I had heard so much about.

Hopman was working with then-junior players such as John McEnroe, Peter Fleming, and Vitas Gerulaitis. He put them on workout courts and made them hit thousands of balls as they ran from side to side and up and back, encouraging them to push themselves to their limits. Very seldom did I hear Hopman talk about certain shot techniques, and when he did, it was always in a way that gave leniency to the player's individual form and style and allowed the player to immediately adapt.

At first I did not understand Hopman's approach. After three months of working with him, however, I started to realize the genius of this man who knew how important it was to train the inner part of an athlete, rather than merely the technical skills. I think what Hopman gave premier athletes with a bit of rebellion in them (such as McEnroe, Fleming, and Gerulaitis) was discipline and a tremendous pride that came from their hard work. Seeing how this pride grew was a great help to me as I developed my own coaching methods.

I later realized there was even more to Hopman's coaching than that. I began asking myself questions about teaching and playing styles. Why were the strokes of the top 10 players in the world so completely different? Why were some players baseline players, and why were others net rushers? Why did almost all the players use different grips to hit the ball?

I thought of all the coaches who were teaching structured styles and forcing their pupils to play in certain ways. Then I would watch Hopman. I saw how he could coax the inner part of a player to get the results that he wanted, but always in a unique way, suiting each player's personality.

During that year, a young Swedish player named Bjorn Borg was quickly coming to international attention. Borg had a revolutionary style that included extremes for stroking on both the forehand and backhand sides. Very few players had ever used a two-handed backhand before, and very few players had ever strayed far enough to use the severe western forehand grip that Borg used. At that point, no one knew the impact that Borg would have on the tennis world. As I watched him play, I wondered if someone had actually taught him those strokes. Did someone tell him to hold the racquet as he did and to hit two-handed, and to loop the ball with such heavy top spin? Or, did he develop the strokes on his own?

Borg would later state that he patterned his strokes after his style of playing table tennis. This made me believe that while certain fundamental skills are important to deliver a ball with the right force, spin, and direction, a player's strokes are developed pretty much according to temperament and individual style. This was a revelation for me as a coach, and it gave me new insight in training players. I realized Hopman's genius more than ever.

Forcing a certain structure on athletes may be confusing to them, and often keeps their outer and inner selves from "meeting," thus preventing them from reaching their full potential. As coaches, we may train athletes in a certain way and drill fundamentals into their heads, but unless they experience the freedom to develop their own unique style, they will not reach their full potential.

I have often wondered what would happen if a coach provided no instruction, but instead delivered thousands of balls to a very coordinated athlete to hit with different strokes. Would the athlete develop into a fine player? Probably so, if the stroke fundamentals become mechanically sound.

Fundamentals are very important, however, and just hitting balls is not enough. In the early stages of development, strict attention must be paid to fundamentals — helping players execute the forehand, backhand, serve, volley, approach shot, return serves, passing shots, and overhead shots. Only when players are able to execute these will they be able to develop an individual style of play and shot delivery.

Providing instruction to a tennis player is like providing instruction to a painter or musician. Painters and musicians learn the fundamentals of fingering and brush work, but artists only become artists when they are able to give physical expression to the world inside themselves. It is the same with tennis players. Athletics is one of the purest forms of art. It is tragic when an athlete's inner self is inhibited by a coach's teaching methods, or at the other extreme, a coach's lack of knowledge of the fundamentals that would have provided the athlete with the tools to become an artist.

Coaches must understand that their players will perform according to their personalities. A conservative person will have a conservative style of play, just as a reckless person will have a reckless style of play. It is interesting that in critical match situations, players will do exactly what their personality dictates.

A coach's most important job is to merge the athlete's outer and inner selves. This union is the key to whether or not players reach their potential. Coaches should spend about 90 percent of their time in the early stages of a player's development working on technical skills and fundamentals. As a player develops a solid base of skills, the coach should work 50 percent on fundamentals and 50 percent on the mental and emotional aspects of competition. As fundamentals become ingrained, nearly a complete range of freedom should be given to the athlete to play from the inside out as temperament dictates, with the coach keeping a watchful eye on technical flaws that may prevent the athlete from progressing.

Finding Your Stroke

If you look at the playing styles of the top 10 players in the world, either women or men, you seldom see the exact same strokes. Every player has his or her own style — from meticulous to flamboyant, from smooth and compact to large and sweeping. The stroke patterns are as unique as each player's personality, and reflect that personality. What makes each player's strokes successful, though, are the same laws of physics and biomechanics: the use of the big muscle groups of the body to supply torque and force for racquet head speed, timing to transfer that force to the ball, and the small muscle groups of the hands for direction and spin.

Simply put, I tell my students to use their legs, trunk and body as the motor to supply power for racquet head speed, while the hands are the steering wheel that give direction, spin, and placement to the ball. These two components combine to supply good biomechanics for the player.

I have drills that teach the players to get effortless power from their legs while they attempt to hit balls from one fence to the other fence with a smooth stroke. As their shots start reaching the opposite fence, I tell the players to start using their hands and touch to gradually control the ball and place it on the court while still getting the same power into the ball. When players miss, I remind them that the stroke is for power and the hands are for direction; or, the stroke is the motor, the hands are the steering wheel. Do not change your stroke as long as you're getting plenty of effortless power through the ball; work to train the hands and timing to control the racquet and direct that power.

The hand-timing takes the longest for players to master. Good biomechanics for power should be stressed and locked in as early as possible in the training progress so that a fundamental base is always there.

I believe this simple approach to teaching the strokes makes it easier for players to improve quickly without being slowed by over-analysis whenever they miss a shot. The term "paralysis by analysis" is very appropriate for some people, especially adults who take up the game later in life. They simply make the game much harder than it should be.

Understand, good mechanics for strokes are important, as is developing a fundamentally sound style. But hundreds of balls must be hit to train the hands and timing skills. These are universal principles for tennis.

The point is this: keep it simple and play the game according to your unique personality. The mechanics of hitting the ball should be basic and consistent. An instructor can help you train your muscle memory through practice until your stroke becomes automatic. But when you compete, you must incorporate those mechanics into your own style of play. Remember, you are No. 1 in the world at your individual style. Use it.

The Tool Box of Skills

The development of tennis skills should follow a logical progression, beginning with consistency and progressing to placement, depth, spin, and then power (see figure 5-1).

Becoming consistent with the most basic shots is the first step, and placing balls consistently from corner to corner follows. Next is the ability to use both under-spin and top-spin as deep balls are hit consistently to each corner, and last is the ability to add power to those shots.

Most players work on bits and pieces of each of these skills throughout their development, but it is important to understand that each skill builds on the previous skills. Many players try to learn power before they learn the other skills that are necessary to control the ball. This will only work if players are willing to hit hundreds of balls to harness power and maintain consistency. I often tell my players that they key to each stroke is to hit the best shot they can hit without making an error. If you hit a more aggressive shot, you need a safer target. If you hit an easier shot, you can use more precise targets.

Consistency is the ability to get the ball back and into the opponent's court time and time again. This should be a player's first goal as a new stroke is learned. The true measure of consistency is how well the stroke holds up under pressure.

Placement is the ability to hit the ball where you want to within the court. Doing this gives the player the control needed to run the opponent or to direct the ball to a specific place on the court for a point-winning shot.

Depth is the ability to keep an opponent deep in the court. This increases shot-making options, and prevents the opponent from taking the offensive. Controlling depth also may refer to the player's ability to hit short balls and bring the opponent purposely to the net from time to time.

The ability to place *spin* on the ball while maintaining control of the shot is crucial. Being able to hit a ball with top-spin, under-spin, or even side-spin opens multiple dimensions of the game. Not only does it enable a player to control a ball hit aggresssively, it delivers shots the opponent does not like to hit.

Power is the ability to win points outright and to force an opponent into errors. It is exciting and enjoyable to have power, but it should be the last skill to be developed. The elements that dictate power are speed of the racquet head from efficient mechanics of the legs and trunk and good hand timing.

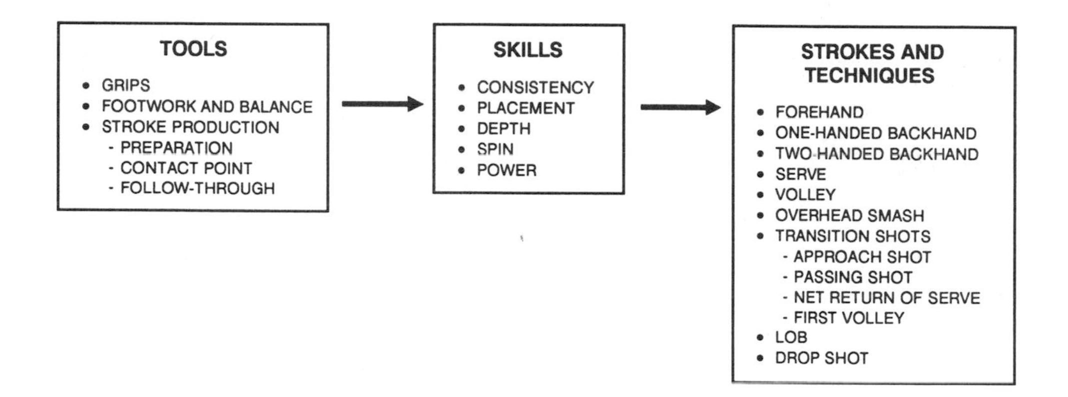

Figure 5-1. Learn your strokes from the inside-out.

Grips

There are nearly as many ways of holding a tennis racquet as there are people playing the game. Although each player should learn the fundamentals of grip and stroke technique, each person's style and grip will eventually be as unique as his or her signature.

Tennis instructors and coaches are often too rigid in their teaching of grip. As in golf, in which different clubs — and sometimes different grips and swings — are required for each shot, tennis sometimes requires variations from your standard style. Different court surfaces and conditions might demand different hitting zones. Clay courts provide a slow, high bounce; hard concrete or asphalt courts provide a medium height and medium-paced bounce; and gym floors or grass courts provide a very low, very fast bounce. For each surface, a variation from your standard style might be needed to hit the ball for the best impact and leverage. The surface on which a player learns to play often dictates the grip uses most.

Each player usually has a favorite grip. Sometimes, though, balls are high, sometimes low, sometimes wide and away, and sometimes close to the player. Some are fast, some are slow, and almost all are delivered with a different spin. To use the same grip for all shots, a player would have to move fast enough to set up for each shot every time. This is often possible on ground strokes, where a player has time to judge the bounce, but not on volleys.

Novice players become comfortable with a particular grip, usually based on the court surface they are accustomed to. As their skills develop and they learn to hit balls of different heights and speeds, it becomes possible to vary the grip when having to hit from a difficult position. Players should choose grips that enable them to make contact with the ball in the optimal strike zone.

Four basic grips are used by probably 90 percent of the world's players, including the professionals. They are the continental, the eastern, the semi-western, and the western grips. Figure 5-2 shows the approximate contact zone for each grip for the forehand. The experienced player will learn that for shots other than the forehand, a slightly different grip and hand position may be used for maximum effectiveness. More than one grip is acceptable for each stroke.

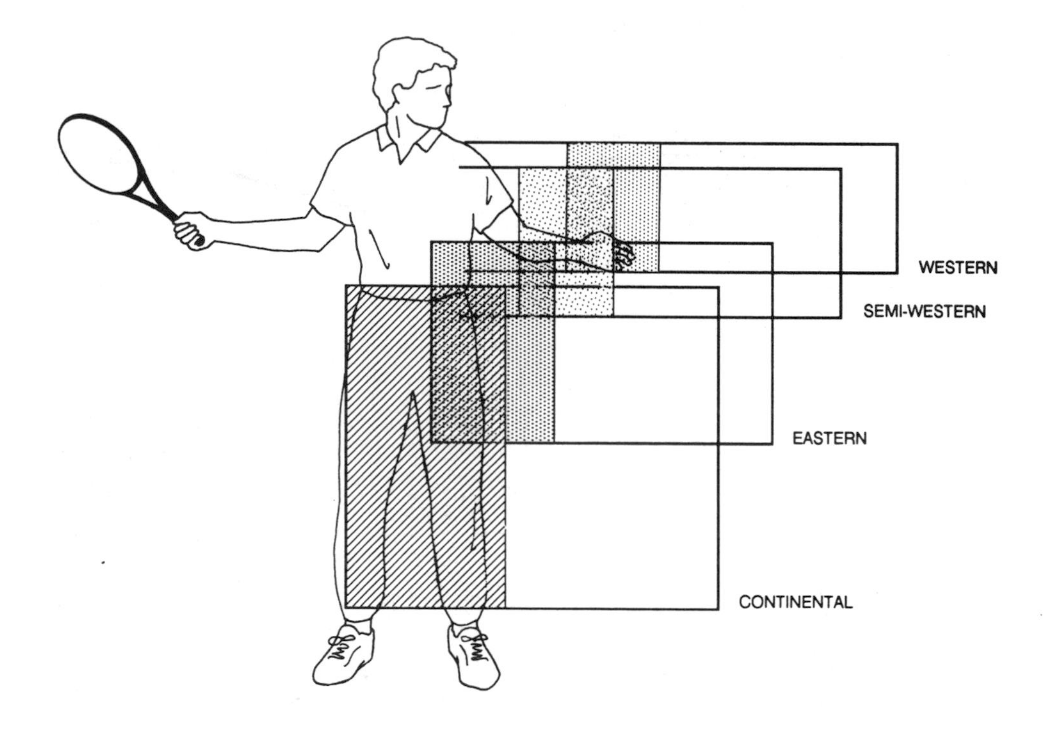

Figure 5-2. Approximate contact zones for different forehand grips.

The following photographs illustrate the grips and show a player using each grip to hit a forehand in a different contact zone.

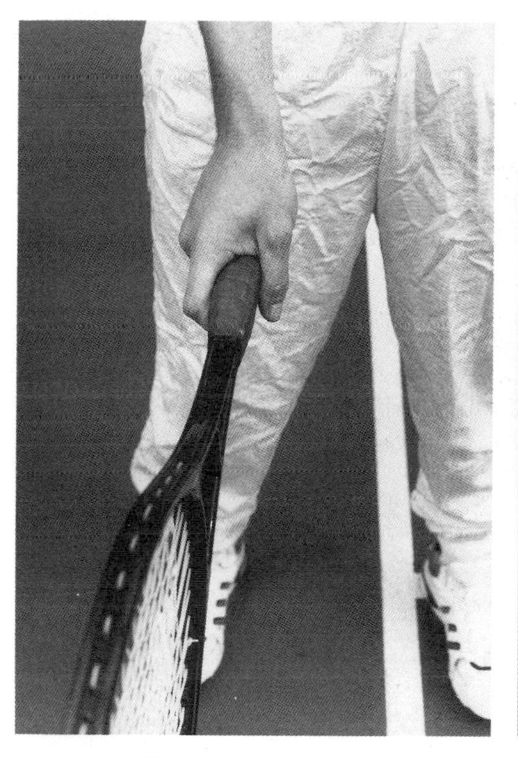

Continental grip.

Continental grip contact point.

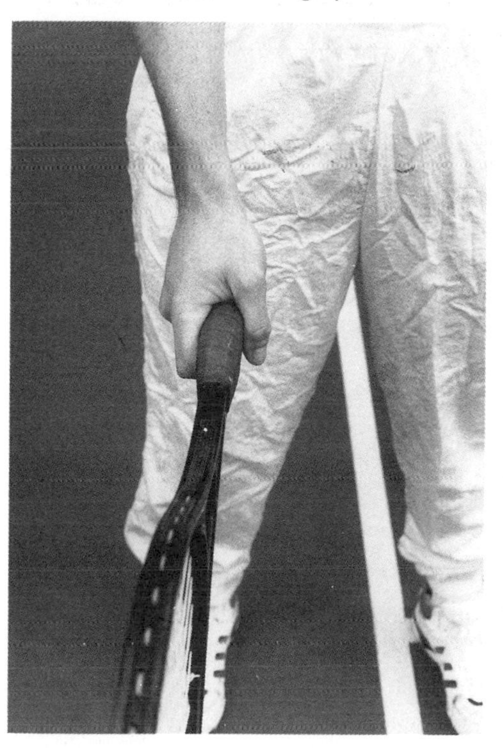

Eastern grip.

Eastern grip contact point.

Semi-western grip.

Semi-western grip contact point.

Western grip.

Western grip contact point.

Footwork and Balance

Stroke technique and proper grip are effective only if the player gets into position to use them. Proper footwork and balance are essential.

Two things are important to maintain good balance and leverage when hitting any stroke: the head should be kept down and both feet should be on the ground. Keeping the head down enables good control of the entire body; if the head comes up, so will the arms, legs, and the rest of the body, thereby preventing optimal balance, leverage, and weight transfer through the ball.

The two variations of footwork that are used for all strokes are the closed stance and the open stance. The upper body position is the same for both stances, with the shoulders and side turned in a coiled position sideways to the net. The lower body position varies somewhat, as the closed stance enables the player to step into the ball for linear power. In the closed stance both feet are somewhat perpendicular to the net, while in the open stance the feet are more parallel to the net, therefore allowing the hips full range of turning for circular power.

When moving to the right, the right foot should be the anchor foot that reaches to set up the ball and is then used to pivot for either an open or closed stance. When moving to the left, the left foot becomes the anchor foot.

Closed stance — forehand. *Open stance — forehand.*

Stroke Production

The key to preparation for any stroke in tennis is to turn the shoulders sideways to the net as soon as possible. The shoulders and racquet should move together like a coil or whip, so that the force can be transferred into the racquet head and through the ball. If a player turns and coils the shoulders, the racquet automatically goes back. Leverage on the stroke can easily be lost if the racquet goes back but the shoulders do not turn to coil.

On ground strokes, where leverage for racquet head speed is needed, a player should concentrate on turning the shoulders and coiling the hips to enable the uncoiling action to generate racquet head speed. For stroke leverage on the backswing, the player should move the racquet and shoulders, and then the hips. On the foreswing, the hips move first, followed by the shoulders and finally the racquet.

The contact point varies somewhat for each stroke and each grip, but the general principle is the same: it must be the point where maximum leverage can be achieved. In general, though, the ball must be hit in front of or slightly off the front foot or the line of the body. Weight must be shifted from the back foot to the front foot in order to generate force through the ball.

Proper follow-through. *Short, cramped follow-through.*

Follow-through

The ball is far away from the strings of the racquet when the follow-through is taking place, but the follow-through should be observed to show how a ball is hit. It is important to note the movement of the racquet head, because where it finishes shows where it has been and how it started.

A follow-through that is too high perhaps delivers too much top-spin and a short ball, whereas a follow-through that is too low places too much slice on the ball. A long follow-through usually indicates a longer stroke that produces a deeper ball.

The follow-through also indicates a player's confidence level. A shortened, jerky, or rushed follow-through usually indicates that a player is pressing. A smooth follow-through shows confidence, control, and trust in the stroke. The best stroke enables the racquet head to accelerate and release through impact with little effort or strain by the player.

THE SHOTS OF TENNIS

The flight of a tennis ball after a racquet hits it is determined by the laws of physics. It is important for a player to understand these laws to be more aware of the physical elements of stroke production.

Generally, the ball will only go where the racquet directs it. The speed of the racquet head determines the pace of the ball, and the angle of the stroke upon contact determines the type of spin.

The Forehand

The continental and western grips are the most difficult grips to adjust to hit balls of different heights. The continental grip is best suited for hitting low balls and is difficult to use to hit high balls. The opposite is true with the western grip. Both the eastern and the semi-western grips are more adaptable to low or high balls.

A player using an eastern grip has very few problems adjusting for a low ball and only moderate difficulty adjusting for a high ball. The player using the semi-western grip has little difficulty adjusting to a high ball and only minor difficulty adjusting to a low ball. The hardest thing to do is to make an adjustment from the continental range to the western range and vice-versa.

The proper execution of the forehand is shown in the photographs on the following page.

Shoulders and hips turn and coil as the racquet comes back.

Racquet extends and releases to a position from above to below the ball.

Racquet moves from low to high, and contact point is in front of the body.

The follow-through is long and extended.

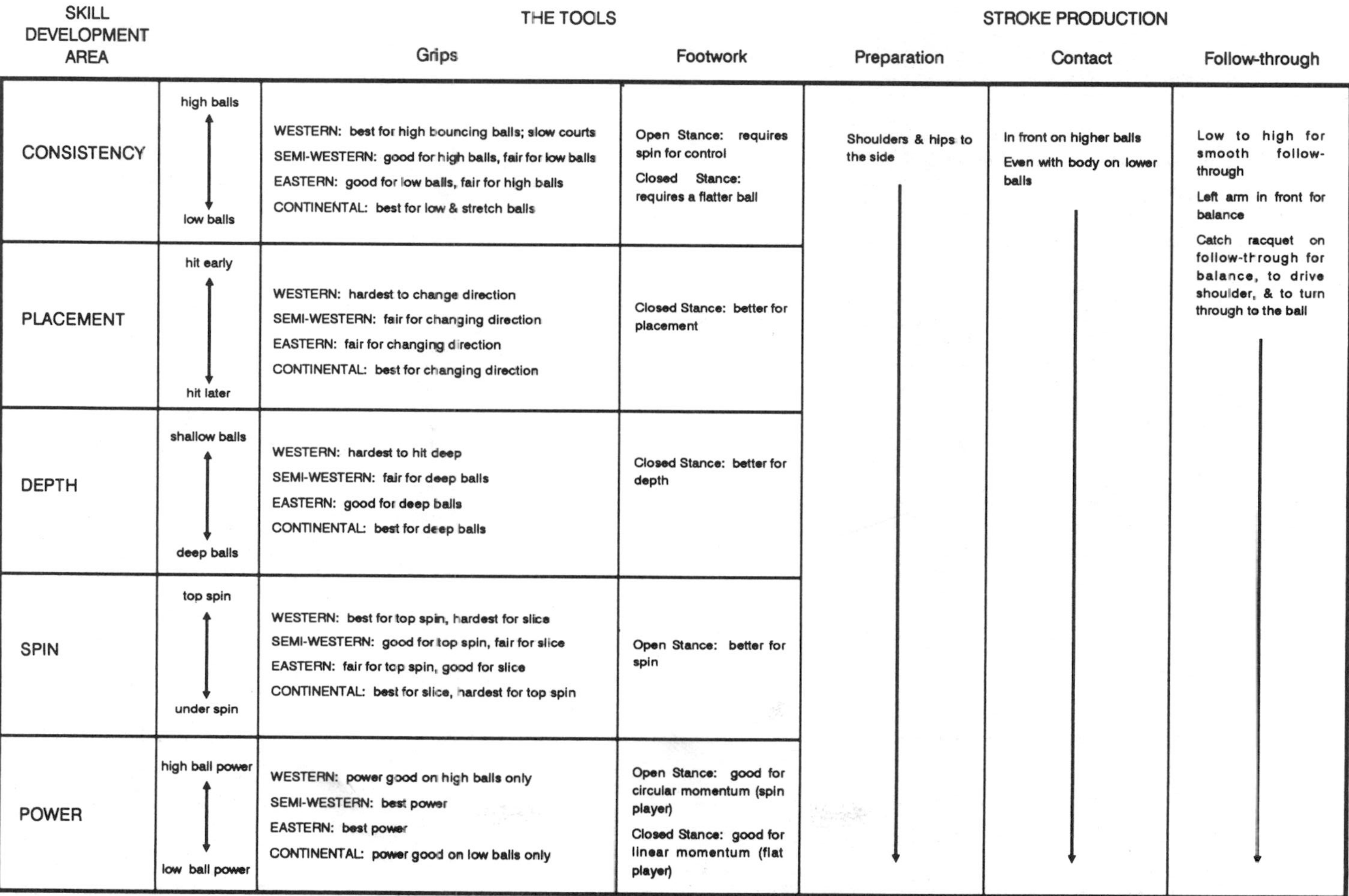

SKILL DEVELOPMENT AREA		THE TOOLS: Grips	THE TOOLS: Footwork	STROKE PRODUCTION: Preparation	STROKE PRODUCTION: Contact	STROKE PRODUCTION: Follow-through
CONSISTENCY	high balls ↕ low balls	WESTERN: best for high bouncing balls; slow courts SEMI-WESTERN: good for high balls, fair for low balls EASTERN: good for low balls, fair for high balls CONTINENTAL: best for low & stretch balls	Open Stance: requires spin for control Closed Stance: requires a flatter ball	Shoulders & hips to the side	In front on higher balls Even with body on lower balls	Low to high for smooth follow-through Left arm in front for balance Catch racquet on follow-through for balance, to drive shoulder, & to turn through to the ball
PLACEMENT	hit early ↕ hit later	WESTERN: hardest to change direction SEMI-WESTERN: fair for changing direction EASTERN: fair for changing direction CONTINENTAL: best for changing direction	Closed Stance: better for placement			
DEPTH	shallow balls ↕ deep balls	WESTERN: hardest to hit deep SEMI-WESTERN: fair for deep balls EASTERN: good for deep balls CONTINENTAL: best for deep balls	Closed Stance: better for depth			
SPIN	top spin ↕ under spin	WESTERN: best for top spin, hardest for slice SEMI-WESTERN: good for top spin, fair for slice EASTERN: fair for top spin, good for slice CONTINENTAL: best for slice, hardest for top spin	Open Stance: better for spin			
POWER	high ball power ↕ low ball power	WESTERN: power good on high balls only SEMI-WESTERN: best power EASTERN: best power CONTINENTAL: power good on low balls only	Open Stance: good for circular momentum (spin player) Closed Stance: good for linear momentum (flat player)			

Figure 5-3. Physical relationships of the forehand.

The Backhand

The one-handed and the two-handed backhands both are accepted and used by players of all abilities.

The one-handed backhand is used in the same situation as the continental or eastern forehand grips. It was developed by grass court or fast court players because it works well with low hard balls or when the player is stretched out. The two-handed backhand is used to hit higher, bouncing balls that are closer to the body; it works well for clay court or slow court players.

Ideally, a player should be versatile enough to use a one-hander for low, skidding balls and for balls away from the body, and also for approach shots and drop shots. The two-hander could be used more as an offensive weapon when the ball is sitting up and easy to make contact with.

Figure 5-4 lists and describes these relationships in more detail.

Backhand grips

The one-handed backhand can be hit well with either the eastern grip or the continental grip. The eastern grip enables a wrist angle that favors a ball hit with top spin or stroked low to high. The continental grip makes it easy to slice the ball or to hit a flatter shot. Although some players can generate top spin using the continental grip, proper leverage with this grip is difficult, which can make it quite difficult to control.

The two-handed backhand enables the player to hit the same balls as the western and semi-western forehand — high balls and offensive shots when the ball is sitting up. With this stroke, the left side of the body of a right-handed player does most of the work, so the grip used with the left hand is of prime importance. The left hand should be placed above the right hand, and an eastern or semi-western grip should be used with the left hand.

Although the power for the stroke does not come from the right hand or the right side of the body, the right hand should grip the racquet with an eastern backhand or a continental grip; this grip will help when a player stretches to hit wide, low, and other out-of-position balls that force a one-handed grip to be used.

The complete stroke is very similar to the left-handed forehand in that it enables the shoulders to rotate through the ball for circular power. It is different from the one-handed backhand, where the left side of the body freezes to shift leverage to the right, which generates linear power.

The photographs on the next page show the proper grips for the eastern backhand grip and the two-handed backhand grip. The photographs on the two following pages show the proper execution of the one-handed backhand and the two-handed backhand.

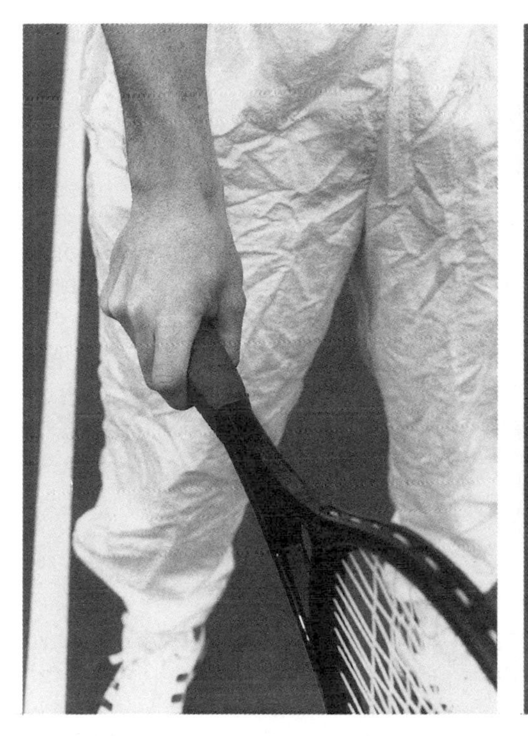

Eastern backhand grip.

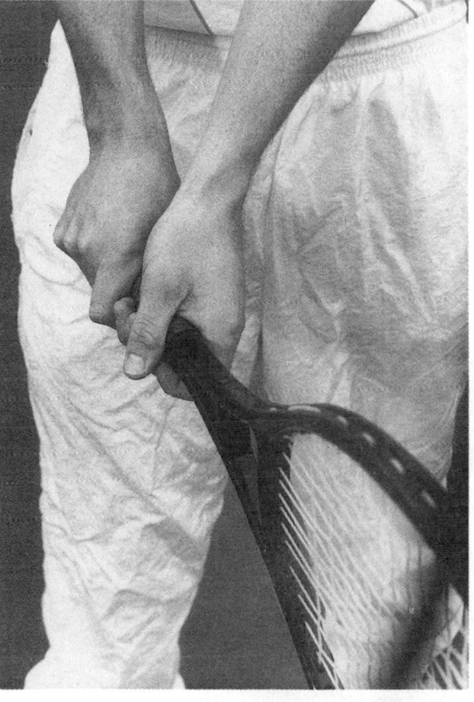

Two-handed backhand grip.

Preparation for backhand slice.

Follow-through on backhand slice.

Shoulders and hips turn and coil
as racquet comes back.

Racquet head extends,
with wrist in a cocked position.

Forward racquet movement
is released from low to high.

Follow-through is long and extended,
shoulders are sideways to the net.

Shoulders and hips coil.

Racquet head extends and releases.

Contact point.

Follow-through.

SKILL DEVELOPMENT AREA		THE TOOLS		STROKE PRODUCTION		
		Grips	Footwork	Preparation	Contact	Follow-through
CONSISTENCY	high balls ↕ low balls	TWO-HANDED: best for high balls ONE-HANDED Eastern: fair for high balls Continental: best for low and wide balls	Closed stance: best for consistency	Shoulders & hips to the side ↓	High balls and two-handers to the front Slice is met further back for more control ↓	Two-handed: shoulders rotate through the ball with high extension, follow-through as if hitting a left-handed forehand One-handed: left arm & left side of body freeze, shifting the leverage or force to the right side of the body ↓
PLACEMENT	hit early ↕ hit later	TWO-HANDED: difficult to change direction ONE-HANDED Eastern: fair for changing direction Continental: better for changing direction	Closed stance: best for placement			
DEPTH	shallow balls ↕ deep balls	TWO-HANDED: difficult to hit deep ONE-HANDED Eastern: fair or good for deep balls Continental: best for deep balls	Closed stance: best for depth			
SPIN	top spin ↕ slice	TWO-HANDED: best for top spin ONE-HANDED Eastern: good for top spin Continental: best for slice	Open stance: can be used for under spin Closed stance: for top spin			
POWER	high ball power ↕ low ball power	TWO-HANDED: circular power for high balls ONE-HANDED Eastern: linear power for high & low balls Continental: linear power for lower balls	Closed stance: best for one-handed and linear power			

Figure 5-4. Physical relationships of the backhand.

Flat serve. *Slice serve.* *Top-spin serve.*

The Serve

The serve is the most important shot in tennis. It is used in every point, and is the only shot that is not affected by the opponent's shot. Its proper execution can make a person progress to a higher level of play.

Service grips

Players can adjust their grips for serves as they progress. Beginning players might want to use the eastern forehand grip, because it enhances consistency and placement. A continental grip, and then an eastern grip, should be used in later stages of development, however, because they enhance depth, spins, and power. The backhand grip is best for the serve, as it enables the wrist pronating action that produces the most varieties of spin as well as greater racquet head speed. However, the continental grip is suitable for most serves, and many advanced and novice players do not advance beyond the continental grip.

Service deliveries

Most advanced players learn at least three deliveries of the serve: a flat serve, a slice (or side-spinning) serve, and a top-spin serve (see photos on previous page). The flat service motion is basic and compact. The slice serve is hit as if you are trying to cut off a section of the ball with your wrist action. The racquet head is positioned as if hammering a nail into the ceiling, with the baby finger leading and the wrist pronating upon contact. With the top-spin serve, contact is made by hitting upward between the 12 o'clock and 1 o'clock position on the ball. Some advanced players become adept at the American twist serve. It is hit with a hard upward brushing action from the wrist.

Torque and power are delivered in the serve in much the same way they are delivered in the forehand and backhand ground strokes. The legs, shoulders, and hips coil and, as they release, the left side of the body freezes to transfer all the force to the racquet side of the body.

Most good servers keep their left arm up for as long as possible, and then bring it into their midsection at contact. This freezes the left side, therefore accelerating the power to the right side for racquet head speed.

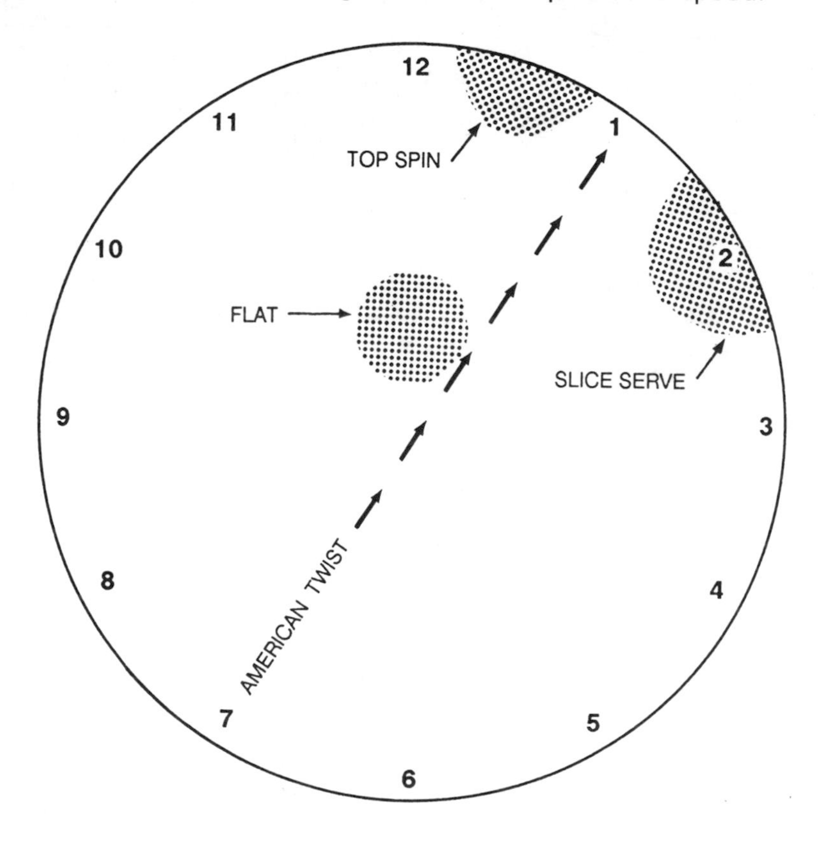

Figure 5-5. Approximate contact points for the four service deliveries.

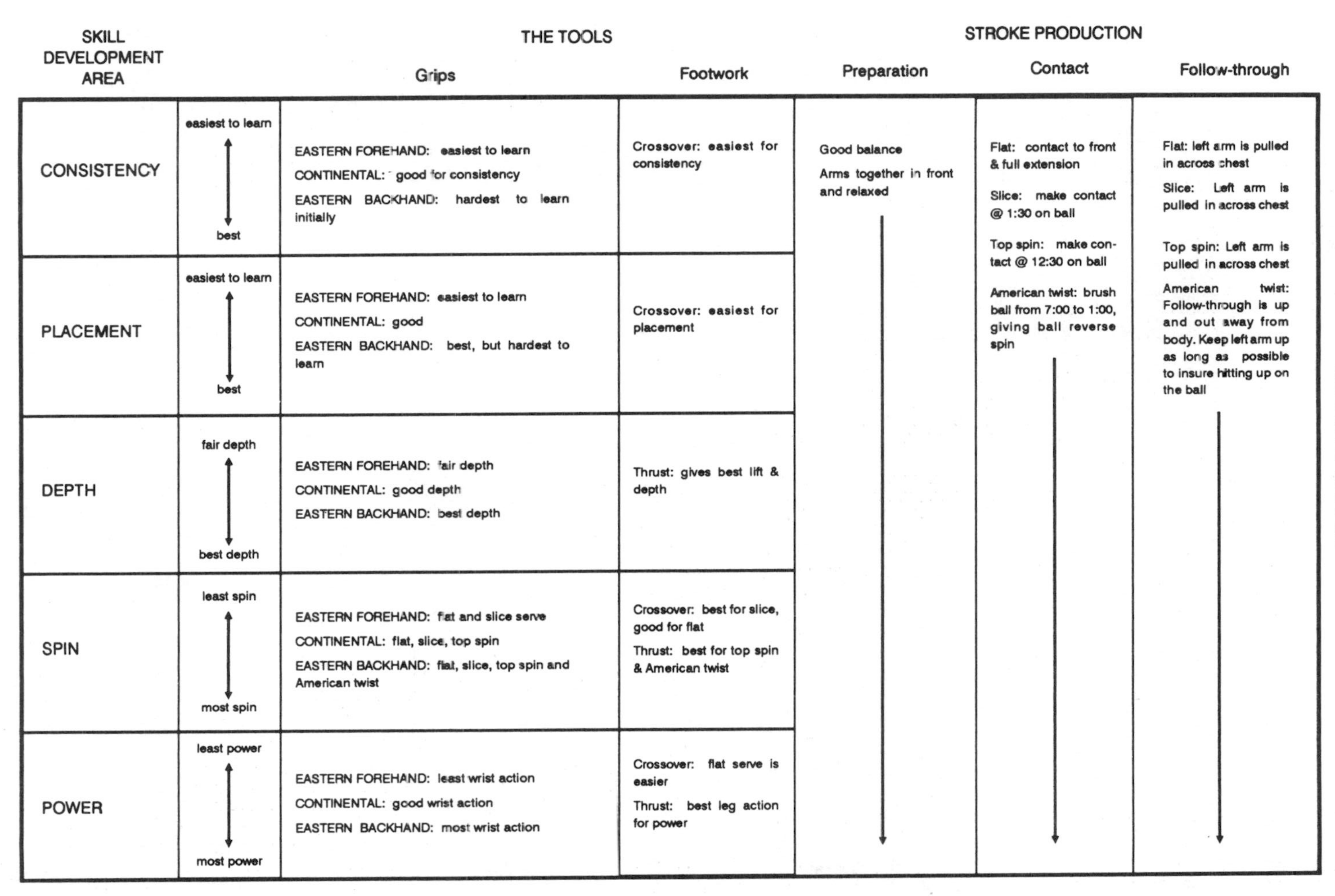

SKILL DEVELOPMENT AREA	THE TOOLS			STROKE PRODUCTION		
		Grips	Footwork	Preparation	Contact	Follow-through
CONSISTENCY	easiest to learn ↕ best	EASTERN FOREHAND: easiest to learn CONTINENTAL: good for consistency EASTERN BACKHAND: hardest to learn initially	Crossover: easiest for consistency	Good balance Arms together in front and relaxed ↓	Flat: contact to front & full extension Slice: make contact @ 1:30 on ball Top spin: make contact @ 12:30 on ball American twist: brush ball from 7:00 to 1:00, giving ball reverse spin ↓	Flat: left arm is pulled in across chest Slice: Left arm is pulled in across chest Top spin: Left arm is pulled in across chest American twist: Follow-through is up and out away from body. Keep left arm up as long as possible to insure hitting up on the ball ↓
PLACEMENT	easiest to learn ↕ best	EASTERN FOREHAND: easiest to learn CONTINENTAL: good EASTERN BACKHAND: best, but hardest to learn	Crossover: easiest for placement			
DEPTH	fair depth ↕ best depth	EASTERN FOREHAND: fair depth CONTINENTAL: good depth EASTERN BACKHAND: best depth	Thrust: gives best lift & depth			
SPIN	least spin ↕ most spin	EASTERN FOREHAND: flat and slice serve CONTINENTAL: flat, slice, top spin EASTERN BACKHAND: flat, slice, top spin and American twist	Crossover: best for slice, good for flat Thrust: best for top spin & American twist			
POWER	least power ↕ most power	EASTERN FOREHAND: least wrist action CONTINENTAL: good wrist action EASTERN BACKHAND: most wrist action	Crossover: flat serve is easier Thrust: best leg action for power			

Figure 5-6. Physical relationships of the serve.

Service footwork

The two most accepted service footwork methods are the crossover method and the thrust method. The crossover method is much more easily learned, and is very good for beginners or for players who do not have enough strength in their legs to get leverage from them.When serving with this method, the left foot is kept in place, and the right foot crosses over with the service motion to shift the body weight through the ball. The crossover footwork method is shown in the photographs on the following page.

The thrust method is better for good athletes who can generate power from the coiling action of their legs. The right foot is brought up behind the left as the ball is tossed and the legs coil. The legs then push upward as the body explodes to the ball. Unlike the crossover method, the left foot leads into the court as the player makes contact with the ball, thus enabling the body to stay sideways as the left side freezes, which transfers the force to the right side and into the shot. Staying sideways also forces the athlete to hit up on the ball and get maximum extension. The following photographs show the thrust footwork method.

Thrust footwork.

Thrust follow-through.

Service preparation.

Coiling action and toss.

Extension and contact.

Follow-through, with crossover.

Read the Receiver and Attack the Grips

The server should study the receiver's grip pattern, because the server then can take advantage of the restrictions and liabilities of the different grips. The strategy should be to serve the ball away from the "strike zone" of the receiver's strokes. It is comparable to a pitcher throwing away from a batter's favorite hitting zone. The target areas are as follows:

Serving against the western forehand grip. The western forehand grip is very vulnerable to flat or low balls that are moving away from the body. A slice or hard flat serve that pulls the receiver toward the deuce court often forces the receiver to mis-hit or shank the return.

Serving against the continental forehand grip. The continental grip favors a flat, low ball outside, so a high kicking ball to this forehand is often hard for the receiver to handle. The receiver may be able to block back a shot, but should not be able to hit an offensive return off of this serve.

Serving against the two-handed backhand. Reach is the chief liability of the two-handed backhand. If the serve can be hit with a wide angle, the receiver either will have difficulty making a good return, or will be pulled wide far enough to give the server good court positioning. A poor wide kick, though, enables the receiver to hit a ball from within the strike zone, therefore a low wide ball would be the best delivery to the two-hander. A serve aimed with some slice toward the midsection also works well against the two-hander because it "jams" the receiver, much like an inside curve ball in baseball.

Serving against the one-handed backhand. If the receiver is not very strong, a high serving kick can produce a weak or a floating return.

Figure 5-7. Forehand serving targets and backhand serving targets.

The Volley

The volley is a much easier stroke to learn than the forehand, backhand, and serve, because the movement is less complicated. The problem, however, is that you have less time to prepare for the shot. The continental grip is most adaptable for both the forehand and backhand volleys at nearly all heights and distances from the body.

The ball should be struck with a short blocking motion in front of the body, and the racquet head should be cocked above the wrist. Volleys should be made at eye level. This means that on low volleys, the knees should bend low to keep the racquet head up. The racquet motion is a short wrist press with the feeling of the little finger leading the racquet head toward the target.

Unlike ground strokes, where the coiling action of the shoulders and hips comes first, the first movement a player must make in preparation for the volley is to lay the wrist back so that it is parallel to the net with the racquet head slightly above the wrist to prepare the racquet head for contact. The shoulders are then turned, but the racquet head and hands should stay in front of the body. The weight is then transferred to the front foot via a crossover step, and contact is made in front of the body.

The opposite hand on the forehand volley stays in front of the body. The hands should come together upon impact for more torque. On the backhand, the right shoulder is forward and the left hand goes backward upon impact for balance and torque. The power of the volley should be hit in a linear motion, with the body sideways to the net.

Volley ready position.

First movement — forehand volley.

Forehand volley contact.

Forehand volley follow-through.

First movement — backhand volley.

Backhand volley follow-through.

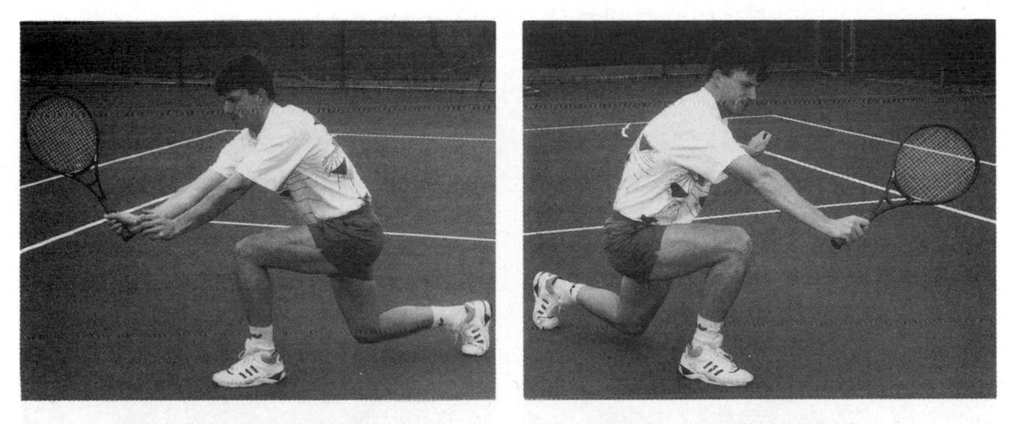

Low forehand volley. *Low backhand volley.*

The Overhead Smash

A player's net game depends heavily on mastering the overhead smash. Opponents usually try to lob the ball over players at the net, so if a player has a good smash, it puts much more pressure on the opponent's passing shot.

The technique of the overhead smash can be simple if basic fundamentals are followed. From a ready position at the net, the racquet head should be moved straight back with a short backswing into a cocked position, the right foot dropped one step backward and the left arm raised to point at the ball. This positions the player so the side of the body faces the net, and enables freedom of movement. When this three-point sequence becomes automatic, the smash should be effective. The grip is the same as used for the serve.

The ball should fall as if it would hit the player in the chest or the forehead if it was not struck. A good drill to help a player learn positioning under a falling ball is to have the player turn sideways with the racquet cocked and the free arm pointing up at the ball. As the ball falls, the player reaches up with the arm fully extended, the hand pointed, and catch the ball. The hitting action is the same as that in the flat serve. The body stays sideways and the ball is hit from a fully extended position at approximately 1 o'clock.

The scissors jump

If possible, both feet should be on the ground when the overhead smash is hit, because this position provides the best balance. If the ball is lobbed well and is too high for the player to stay on the ground, a scissors jump becomes necessary. This forces the player to stay sideways and helps avoid pulling the ball down into the net. Although this action looks complicated, it is actually a very natural movement and is easy to do with some practice. The athlete must move backward quickly in a sideways position, push off the ground with the right foot, and land on the left foot, moving the legs in a scissors motion in the process.

Overhead ready position.

First movement — overhead.

Scissors jump.

Follow-through.

TRANSITION SHOTS

Transition shots enable a change in the style of play during a point. These include the approach shot, the passing shot, the return of serve and the first volley. Except for the return of serve, each of these shots involves a transition from the baseline to the net by one player or the opponent.

Transition shots are the ones most often missed in tennis. Many errors occur because the pattern of play changes and the rhythm of the point is altered. I have a rule for my players that the angle of the return shot not be changed on a transition shot. The timing is tough enough as it is, and to change the direction of the ball into the open part of the court greatly increases the chances of an error or results in a shot the opponent can easily handle.

Returning the ball to where it was hit from (not changing the direction of the ball), enables a player to make a shot that leaves the strings of the racquet at a right angle. This also keeps the court closed and forces the opponent to hit a ball from a poor position, tempting the opponent to hit to the open court or change direction.

Players also should think of hitting two shots when they approach, two shots when they pass, two shots when they return serve, and two shots to volley. This makes them realize that the purpose of a transition shot is to set up the next shot, not to end the point. (Otherwise, it would be called a put-away shot.)

The Approach Shot

In the summer of 1972, I was a summer camp counselor watching Stan Smith and Ilie Nastase play for the Wimbledon championship on television. The camp director, Harry Hopman, also was watching. Mr. Hopman often made a one-sentence comment about tennis or about life that would be so profound that it carved a permanent place in my memory.

Nastase, the great shot-maker, had just been forced into the corner of the court with a great Smith approach shot. On the dead run, Nastase hit a perfect down-the-line backhand passing shot that left Smith diving onto the grass. One of the instructors commented, ''Wow, what a great shot.'' Hopman responded with, ''No, it wasn't, that was the only shot he had.'' That one statement taught spoke volumes about the importance of proper placement on approach shots.

What Hopman meant was that players often are physically able to make great shots, especially if they *have* to make them. In the Wimbledon match, Nastase's back was to the wall, and his shot down the line with the only chance he had. The fact that he made the shot was not a great feat, any more than it is for a basketball player who throws in a long three-pointer out of desperation at the buzzer.

I learned from Hopman that day that an approach shot is just that — a shot that a player makes upong approaching the net. The player's job is to handcuff the opponent *and* to time the delivery of the shot to be able to get into position at the net for the next shot. The ball may be hit short or deep, high or low, to the corner or to the middle, but the main objective is to find a vulnerable area in the opponent's passing shots.

I learned more than that, however. I learned that many times a player forced into a corner can play "spinal cord tennis" — that is, tennis played automatically without thought. Hopman loved the approach shot up the middle because it gave the opponent choices, and having choices is often the undoing of a talented shot-maker like Nastase. Hopman taught me that any opponent can make a great shot after a player goes to the net, but this should never deter the player from pursuing the attacking game.

After a player finds the right approach shot to use, the advantage of better court positioning pays off. Proper execution of the correct approach shots may actually be the quickest way to rapid improvement in a player's game.

As in other strokes, the shoulders turn sideways to the net. As the player moves into position, the anchor foot is placed down (left foot on backhand, right on forehand), and the weight is shifted from the anchor foot, with force exerted through the ball, onto the front foot. The power in approach shots is linear. The stroke is similar to the volley, but with more backswing and follow-through. Under-spin is recommended to keep the delivery low and to give the approaching player time to assume a balanced and ready position.

Note: If top-spin approach shots are used, they are best played up the middle or to the stroke that has the most difficulty with high balls.

Approach shot — ready position.

Approach shot — contact point.

The Passing Shot

This section could be called "Passing Shots," because it usually takes more than one shot to pass. The first shot is to put the opponent at the net off-balance, and the next one is to score the point with a smaller degree of difficulty. A player can attempt a great passing shot on the first attempt, but the percentages are not favorable unless the shot is much better than the opponent covering the net.

To go for the passing shot on the first whack at the ball is comparable to a basketball team that shoots a 30-footer immediately after crossing the 10-second line. When a player uses the first shot to set up the second or third passing shot, it is more like a basketball team that passes the ball two or three times to get a higher percentage shot.

Of course, the best teams can often hit the quick 30-footers as well as pass the ball three or four times to get an easier shot. Likewise, the best tennis players can make great passing shots when they must, but they understand the importance of being able to hit through an opponent once or twice to get the high percentage final passing shot.

The key to effective passing shots is to take the first ball early and return it where it came from without changing the angle of the shot. This should catch the opponent off-balance and force a weak volley that can be returned with an easy passing shot.

The Return of Serve

The return of the serve is perhaps the second most important shot in tennis because, like the serve, it must be used in every point of every other game.

The player returning service is reacting to the opponent, and a good return has very few moving parts. Again, because it is a transition shot, a good general rule is not to change the direction of the ball, thus eliminating many errors that may be caused by trying to make a difficult shot instead of hitting through the opponent. Good returners use their opponent's pace and try to use a short backswing for good weight transfer, and take the ball early and hit the ball where it came from.

Reading a server

Most servers have a serving pattern. For example, the first serve might be flat and to the backhand side and the second serve is a top-spin serve to the backhand. Or, the first serve is wide and the second serve is up the middle.

A good rule to follow for a player returning serve is to watch for the server's pattern for a few games and then gauge the returns accordingly. For example, if the server hits the first serve flat to the backhand side most of the time, the receiving player should be waiting with a backhand grip and in position for a backhand stroke. If the serve is to the backhand, the receiver can make a short low-to-high swing and lean into the ball to produce an excellent return. If the serve is to the forehand side, the receiver still can make a very solid stretch forehand with the backhand grip.

The only serve that would really make the receiver vulnerable would be the high kicker to the forehand, and it is unlikely that the server would try this on a first serve. However, most second serves are kick serves. If this is the case, the receiver can either wait with a forehand grip to move around and smack a forehand, or can slice a backhand from high to low and follow it to the net.

If the receiver is successful in reading the opponent's service delivery, the receiver can disrupt the server's pattern. The server then reacts to the receiver's pattern, thereby giving the receiver a better chance of controlling the tempo of the game.

Technique

As the receiver awaits the serve, the lower body should be relaxed and positioned so that the center of gravity is high. For many years, players were taught that it is best to wait in a very low crouched position with the knees bent and the center of gravity very low. But the laws of physics show that while a lower center of gravity is better for stability (such as a three-point stance for a lineman in football or a four-point stance for a wrestler), a higher center of gravity is better for a quick movement in any direction. John McEnroe has used this stance effectively.

The best technique is to wait in a low position, rise up on the toes for a higher center of gravity, and then lean into the ball with a wide base that provides stability and enables weight transfer into the shot. The upper body movement is quite simple. As the server tosses the ball, the receiver comes up for a higher center of gravity and turns only the relaxed shoulders, to the forehand or backhand position, and then flows forward along the path of the oncoming ball with a short, firm motion.

High-to-low or low-to-high

On a flat, hard first service, it is best for the stroke to flow in a low-to-high arc. Very often a player tries to slice (high-to-low) a hard, fast serve. Although this may feel comfortable and safe, it usually produces a ball in the net or a weak, floating return. A low-to-high arc enables the racquet to hit along the plane of the ball and lift it to clear the net.

However, on a high, kicking serve, the returner should try to hit the ball with a high-to-low arc to bring the ball down into the court. The returner also might want to move around the ball and smack a forehand if possible.

The First Volley

The first volley is considered a transition shot because of its similarity to the approach shot.

Three rules should be followed for the first volley:

- The serving player should try to advance as far as possible into the court after the serve. This provides an opportunity to make an effective first volley. Otherwise, a ball popped up makes it very easy for the returner to pass the server.
- If an outright winner cannot be hit to the open court, the first volley should be hit back to where it came from or to the middle of the court, and the finishing volley should be placed to the open court. This rule is very important, because if a cross-court volley is not put away, the entire court is left open for an easy passing shot by the opponent. In general, on any ball that can be put away, the player should go to the open court. If the ball cannot be put away, the court should be kept closed. I call serve and volley drills *serve and volley-volley* drills, which reminds the players that it takes two shots to volley.
- The net should be closed off after the first volley. If the first volley is effective, the server should be in control of the point. As the ball is in flight, the server should take three or four steps toward the net to close out the point. Not closing off the net is a mistake that gives the opponent an angle to hit a passing shot or a chance to get back into the point.

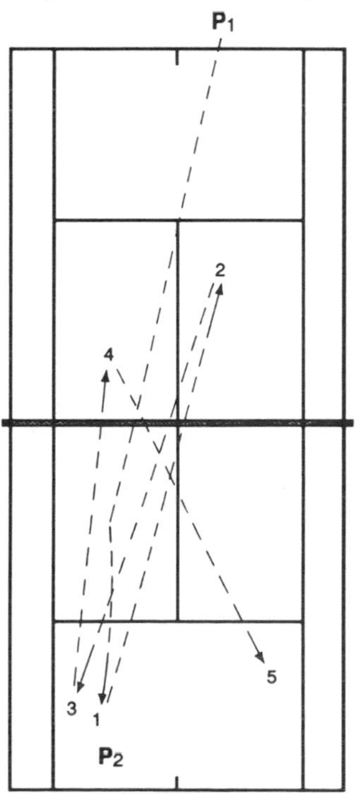

Figure 5-8. The perfect serve-and-volley point. The server (P1) makes a first serve to the opponent's body in the ad court. (1), moves into the service line, volleys a low ball back to where it came from (2 and 3), closes off the net and angles the second volley cross court (4 and 5).

The Lob

The lob is one of the best passing shots to use when the opponent comes to the net. Two kinds are available: the defensive lob and the offensive lob. If the opponent's shot can be controlled, the player should hit an offensive lob as an alternative to a passing shot. If the opponent's shot stretches the player or the player is out of the play, a very high defensive lob should be hit.

Defensive lobs

The defensive lob should be used when a player is out of position and needs time to set up. If the player can get the ball up high enough and back on the baseline, the opponent virtually has to start the point over. The higher defensive lobs are hit the better, because nothing is more difficult than hitting a ball that is falling rapidly. When a player is stretched out, it is a good idea to use a continental grip in order to keep a firm wrist to give leverage for a firm ball.

Offensive lobs

The offensive lob should be used as an option to a passing shot — out of choice, not out of necessity. The player must have complete control of the ball and be able to disguise the shot until the last second. The arc of the ball's flight should be much lower than the arc of the defensive lob, and it also is a good idea to place the lob over the opponent's backhand side, where an overhead would be very difficult.

Players today are quite adept at hitting the top-spin lob, but this shot should be used only when the ball is sitting up enough to use a full swing and a grip that enables a lot of top-spin to be put on the ball.

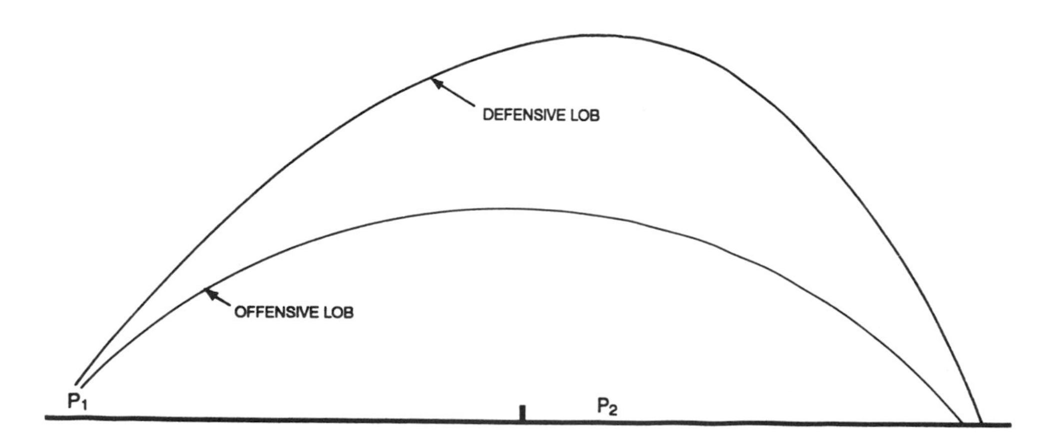

Figure 5-9. The flight paths of the offensive and defensive lobs.

The Drop Shot

One principle for controlling the depth of a shot at strategic times is to hit balls short, thereby forcing the opponent to come to the net. A drop shot is an excellent shot to use to do this, but it must be well-disguised. It should not be used as a defensive shot, only as an offensive tactic. Placement is very important; a poor drop shot is disastrous because it enables the opponent to take immediate charge of the point.

Three rules are important to follow when executing the drop shot:

- A drop shot made from the baseline should be made cross-court. This keeps the court closed so that if the opponent does get to the ball, a passing shot can be made on the next ball.
- A drop shot made from the forecourt should be made in front of you or down the line. This keeps the court closed and provides another play on the ball if the opponent returns the ball.
- The drop shot should be used only as an offensive tactical shot, which makes the opponent react to him. As a desperation shot or a way out of the point, it is one of the worst shots a player can choose.

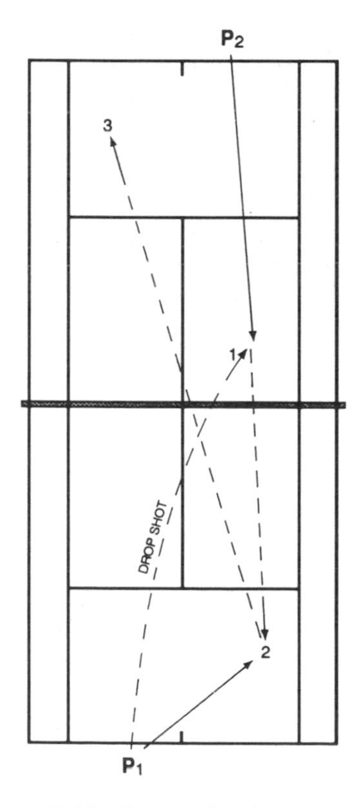

Figure 5-10. From the backcourt, hit drop shots cross-court.

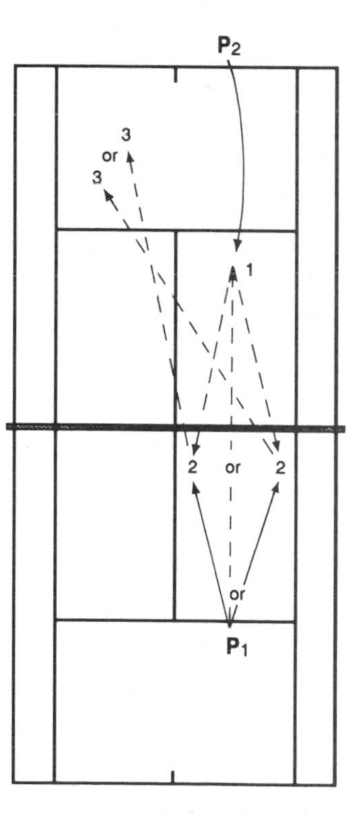

Figure 5-11. From the forecourt, hit drop shots down the line or in front.

The Backboard: Your Best Practice Partner

The beginning player often hesitates to ask people of any level to practice or play out of fear of embarrassment. Fortunately, the best and most reliable practice player is always available: the backboard. The backboard can be any size or surface, as long as it is large enough to provide a suitable target and returns balls with a consistent bounce. Beginning players should use an old ball with a slower bounce to take better control of their rallies.

Just about any skill that a player needs for a match can be learned and developed against a backboard, except handling different spins that may come off of the opponent's racquet. A consistent bounce, though, helps a player develop a steady, reliable stroke.

All strokes and most game situations can be practiced alone or with a partner, but the learning progression explained previously should be used. Use a dead ball that won't bounce back quickly, allowing better technique.

The progression for strokes trained on the backboard is as follows:

1. Consistency. This should be the first goal in learning any stroke. Repetitive work done with a stroke is about the only way to develop some degree of confidence for its execution. To improve consistency, emphasis should be placed on hitting one stroke at a time. After a player can execute the same stroke 20 to 25 times without an error against the backboard, another stroke can be tried. Players also can develop their consistency by alternating between forehand and backhand shots, to simulate game situations.

2. Placement. The ability to place the ball should be learned immediately after consistency. The easiest way to do this is to give yourself the option of a down-the-line or a cross-court shot on the backboard.

The down-the-line shot returns the ball to the same stroke. On the next exchange, the ball should be hit cross-court to the opposite stroke. The following sequence offers a fairly simple progression for developing placement and control of the ball: forehand to forehand down the line then forehand to backhand cross-court, then backhand to backhand down the line and then backhand to forehand for cross-court again.

3. Depth. A long stroke produces a deep ball. This skill may be practiced on the backboard simply by moving back as far as possible while still being able to hit the ball to it. Novice players learn quickly that the only way to get the ball to the backboard is with a long, smooth stroke. Repetition of this technique enables you to transfer the stroke to the court. Your ball will have to bounce three or four times to return to you, but this is fine, because the emphasis is on lengthening the stroke.

4. Spin. Top-spin, under-spin and even side-spin shots can easily be practiced on the backboard. Again, it is more easily done with a dead ball that does not return as quickly to your racquet from the wall. This gives you time to prepare for each shot and produce the proper spin on the ball.

Spin is one of the most important skills to learn, because it enables a player to have more control of the ball and to hit the ball much harder while still maintaining consistency, placement, and depth.

5. Power. After developing consistency, placement, depth and spin, it becomes easy to work on power with the backboard as well. It should be the last skill practiced.

The best way to work on power is to produce a high soft ball off of the wall and then set up for a kill shot from the forehand or the backhand. If you are adept enough to keep the rally going, this alternating sequence should be repeated as many times consecutively as possible.

For every stroke learned, it is important to maintain the sequence of 1) consistency, 2) placement, 3) depth, 4) spin and 5) power.

Hitting the wall

Most players practice ground strokes first when using the backboard. With practice, a player should be able to move close to the wall and keep the ball in the air with volleys and quick half-volley pickups, in which the ball takes a short hop at the player's feet.

The serve also is easily practiced by walking off a distance of 39 feet from the wall (equal to the distance from the base line and the net), and picking a target on the wall at which to aim. Good shots and bad shots alike will rebound back to the server for another attempt.

Even the overhead smash can be practiced by bouncing or hitting the ball off the ground so that it rebounds high off the wall, enabling you to smash it again in front of the wall.

The greatest advantage of the backboard is that it is a dependable and reliable partner for practice any hour of the day. Players can develop any stroke to any level of competency, as long as they are willing to put in the time. Take advantage of this willing practice partner that never swings and misses, never hits the ball over the fence and never gets tired!

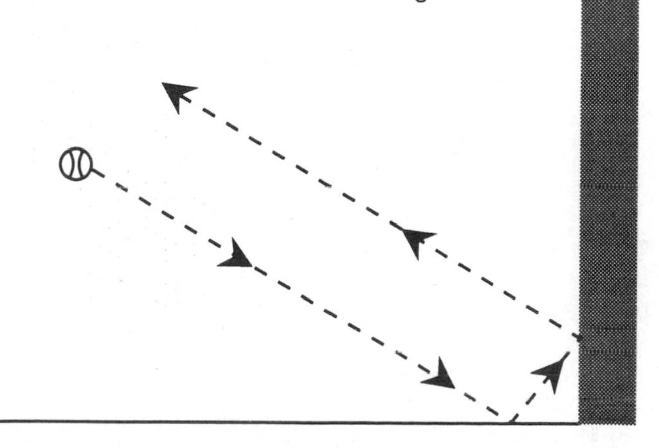

Figure 5-12. Trajectory of ball in practicing overhead smash on the wall.

Harry Hopman was one of the game's greatest teachers.

"The more you sweat in peacetime, the less you'll bleed in war."

— Chinese proverb

6 Drilling Home the Points

After you have developed your stroking patterns on the backboard, you can further improve your skill level by using drills that emphasize the various strokes.

Drills can help you learn new skills and shots that would be difficult to learn by just playing against an opponent, refining them to the point where they can be incorporated into your tool box of skills.

A drill must simulate as closely as possible the shots or situations that occur in a match to be effective. Even the most sophisticated drills do not have merit unless they prepare a player for situations that will be faced in competition. Drills should be simple and specific, with a clear objective.

This section covers the following six groups of drills:

- Feeding drills
- Breakdown or one-on-one rallying drills
- Two-on-one drills
- Match simulation drills
- Serving drills
- Simulated set play

It is not necessary to incorporate all of them into a training program, but a variety should be used so that all of the necessary skills are covered.

Feeding Drills

Feeding drills have the most benefit when a skill is first being learned. They enable a player to focus on and develop a particular shot by returning balls fed to a particular area of the court.

The person feeding the balls should do so with a variety of spins and placement so that the player learns to handle shots of various degrees of difficulty. Although feeding drills instill confidence, it is quite difficult to simulate the spins, power, and rhythm that occur in a game. Each feeding drill should be repeated anywhere from eight to 12 times, depending on the player's fitness and ability.

Wide-Middle Forehand

(See figure 6-1.)

Objective: To work on wide forehands and forehands from the middle position. The major emphasis is on improving movement and setting up for the forehand from any position on the court.

Description: Standing just behind the service line, the coach (C) feeds balls deep and wide to the forehand side (1), making the player (P) stretch to return them. The coach then feeds a ball to the middle (2) so the player has to recover quickly to hit a forehand. The coach continues feeding balls wide (3) and to the middle (4), mixing up the feeds. Balls also should be fed to the backhand corner so that the player can hit inside-out forehands.

Wide-Middle Backhand

(See figure 6-2.)

Objective: To work on wide backhands and backhands from the middle of the court, with the major emphasis on the player's movement and balance in setting up for the shot.

Description: The coach (C) stands behind the service line and feeds a ball wide to the backhand side (1) so the player (P) has to stretch to return it. The coach then feeds a ball to the middle of the court (2), forcing the player to back up into a position to make this backhand shot. The coach continues to hit balls wide (4) and to the middle (3) of the backhand side. As the player becomes more proficient in setting up for each shot, the coach should also feed balls to the forehand side of the court to force the player to develop even better court movement in setting up for balance.

Wide-Middle Volley (Forehand and Backhand)

(See figure 6-3.)

Objective: To work on stretch volleys and volleys from the middle position. The improvement of movement and balance is emphasized.

Description: The coach (C) feeds balls alternately wide and to the middle of the deuce court, forcing the player (P) to stretch for a wide ball (l and 3) and then recover to the middle for a cramped volley (2 and 4). The drill also should be performed with the player in the ad court to work on the backhand volley.

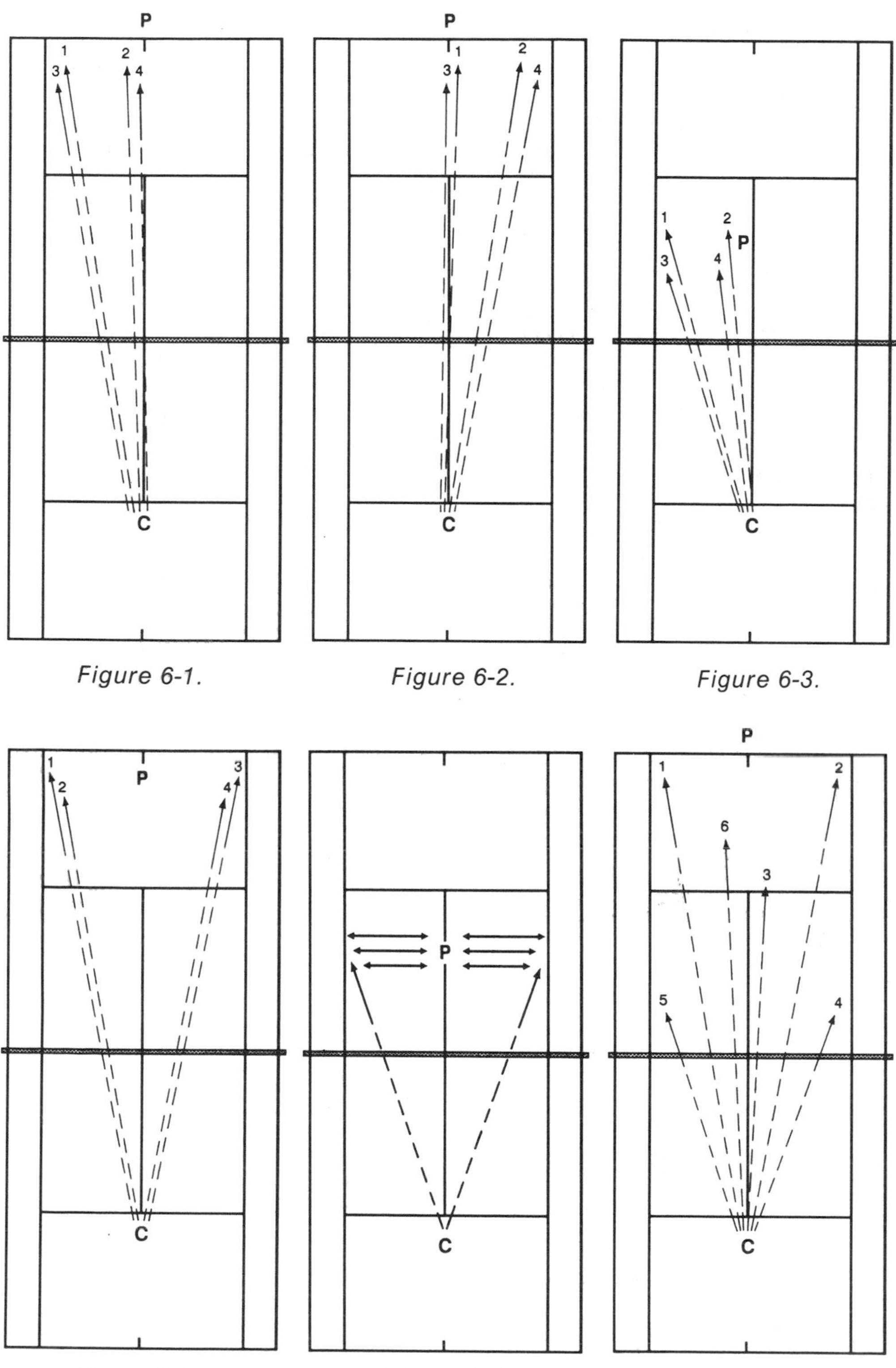

Figure 6-1.

Figure 6-2.

Figure 6-3.

Figure 6-4.

Figure 6-5.

Figure 6-6.

Stretch Ground Stroke

(See figure 6-4.)

Objective: To groove the forehand and backhand while working on footwork and lateral movement.

Description: The coach (C) stands behind the service line and feeds a wide ball to the forehand side of the backcourt (1). The player (P) moves from the center of the backcourt to return the ball, and then recovers to the middle by using good lateral footwork. The coach then feeds the player another wide ball to the forehand side (2) and continues the drill with two consecutive feeds to the backhand side (3 and 4). The player should aim the returns either crosscourt or down the line.

Stretch Volley

(See figure 6-5.)

Objective: To improve movement at the net and to learn how to make the volley when fully stretched out.

Description: The coach (C) stands four to five feet behind the service line and feeds balls to the outstretched reach of the player's (P) forehand and backhand volleys. Special emphasis should be placed on the player's recovering back to the middle after each shot before stretching for the next ball. The player should hit the ball deep to the baseline or make a drop volley.

Six Ball: All-Court Coverage

(See figure 6-6.)

Objective: To combine the stretch forehand and backhand ground strokes with the stretch forehand and backhand volleys.

Description: The coach (C) stands four to five feet behind the service line. Balls are fed to the player (P) so that the player has to move from one corner to the other and stretch to return the balls (1 and 2). The coach then brings the player toward the net by feeding a short ball (3). The player hits the approach shot, and then the coach feeds balls to the player's forehand and backhand sides so the player has to stretch to volley back (4 and 5). The coach can add an overhead as the last shot.

Kill Shot

(See figure 6-7.)

Objective: To develop the player's kill shot, or a shot that is virtually impossible to return.

Description: The coach (C) feeds weak balls to different positions on the court (1, 2, 3, and 4), and the player (P) moves to every ball and hits only a forehand or a backhand. This forces the player to develop footwork and court movement and to learn to hit an aggressive shot off a weak ball. The player should try to hit each shot as aggressively as possible, and shot placement can be made to either corner.

Volley-Close-Smash

(See figure 6-8.)

Objective: To develop forward and backward movement.

Description: The coach (C) feeds a low volley to the feet of the player (P), who starts behind the service line (1). The second volley should be a floater that the player closes on to hit at an angle, and the third shot should be an overhead that the player moves back for and puts away (2 and 3).

Low Ball-High Ball

(See figure 6-9.)

Objective: To work on forward and backward movement and to improve low volleys and overheads.

Description: The player (P) starts behind the service line and moves up quickly to take a short volley out of the air (1). The coach then feeds an immediate overhead beyond the player (2). The player has to move back quickly for a smash (3) and then close again for a short volley (4).

Drop Shot

(See figure 6-10.)

Objective: To improve forward movement for running down drop shots.

Description: The player (P) starts on the baseline. The coach (C) is at the net and drops a very short ball over the net to the right or the left (1 and 2). The player races from the baseline to make the shot, and back pedals to the start again.

Change of Direction (Ground Strokes or Volleys)

(See figure 6-11.)

Objective: To learn how to change the direction of the ball on ground strokes, improve court movement and learn personal limitations.

Description: The coach (C) feeds balls from the deep corner of the court to different places all over the court (1-5). The player gets to every ball and hits shots of different speeds and spins to the opposite corner. This can be done with the player at the net, or with the coach up and the player back, or with both the player and the coach at the net.

No Change of Direction (Ground Strokes and Volleys)

(See figure 6-12.)

Objective: To develop consistency by hitting the ball back from where it came, at a right angle, which is more difficult because the player is trying to change the direction of the ball. The player also learns personal limitations on each ball.

Description: The coach (C) feeds balls from the deep corner or the side net position. The player (P) has to get to every ball (1-5) and hit it back from where it came. This drill can also be done with both the coach and the player up, or with one up and the other back.

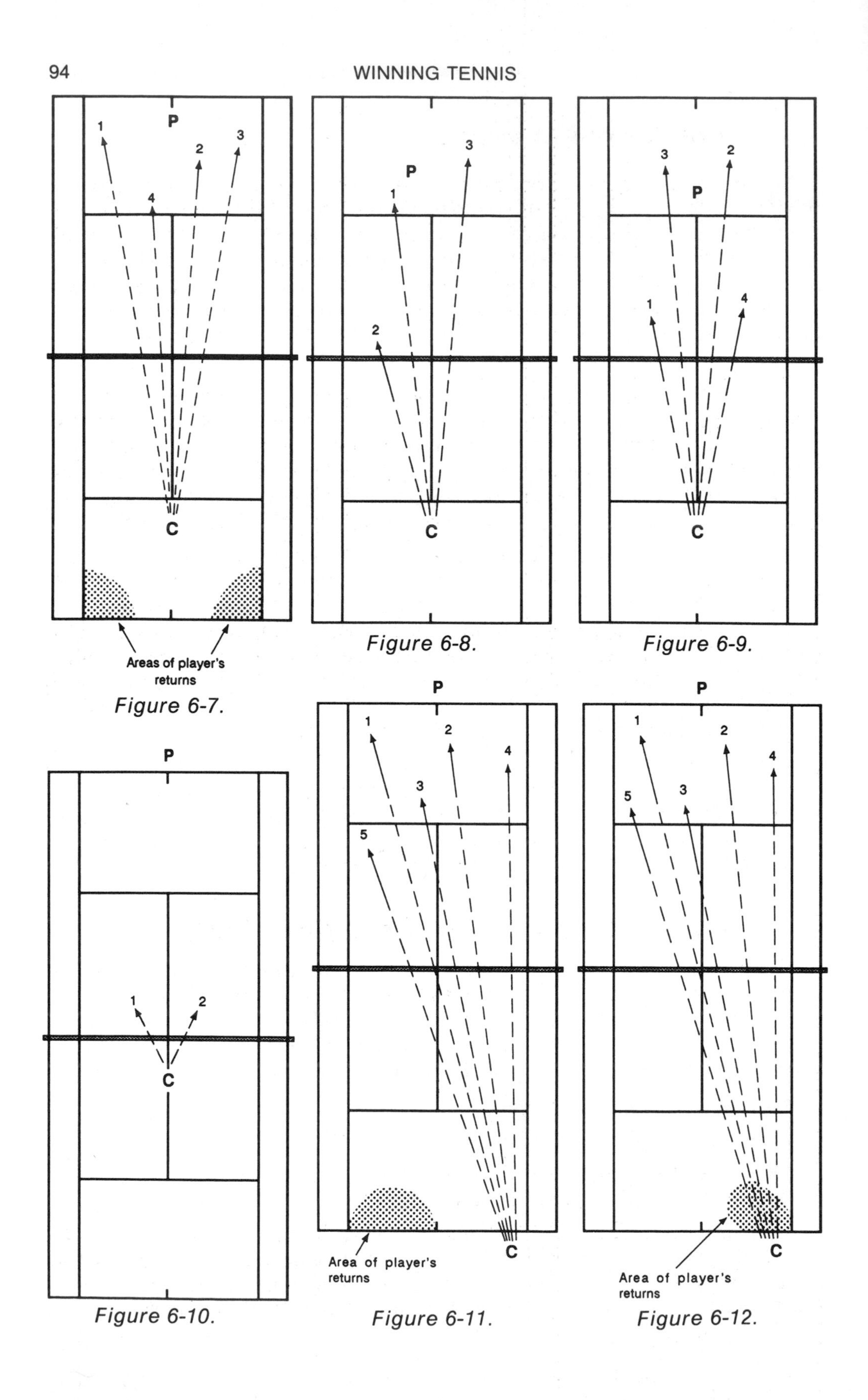

Figure 6-7.

Figure 6-8.

Figure 6-9.

Figure 6-10.

Figure 6-11.

Figure 6-12.

To change, or not to change

During a rally, a player chooses to change or not change the direction of the flight of the ball. Not changing the direction of the ball (hitting the ball back to where it came from) enables the player to hit the ball at a right angle. This is very forgiving to slightly miss-hit shots and also for more difficult shots such as the return of serve, first volleys, passing shots, approach shots, and balls placed so that a player is stretched and becomes off-balance or out of position to return them. Players should not change the direction of the ball on any shot that cannot be controlled.

Changing the direction of the ball (hitting the ball to the open court) is a much riskier proposition. Only a slight change in the angle of the racquet face can misdirect a ball out of bounds or into the net. The temptation is to hit the ball to the open court, away from the opponent. However, this is not always a good idea because of the greater chance for error and because a poorly-hit ball will sit up, thereby giving the opponent an opportunity to put the shot away.

Of course, put-aways usually have to be hit to the open court, or with a change of direction. The key is for a player to recognize personal limitations with each ball hit in a rally, whether the player is in the backcourt or at the net. If the shot cannot be adequately controlled or put away for a winner, the direction of the ball should not be changed. Returning the ball back to where it came from keeps the player in position for the next ball, thereby making it difficult for the opponent to hit a point-winner. If the ball can be controlled or put away, though, the player should hit it to the open court.

Players who compete on extremely fast courts quickly learn that few or no changes in direction can be made. Also, against extremely hard hitters, it is an excellent tactic not to change the direction of the ball, because errors will be reduced and the player can take advantage of the opponent's pace. It also may tempt the hard hitter to go for the open court too often.

Breakdown (One-on-One) Rallying Drills

The following rallying drills teach players how and when to change direction on a shot. In these drills, the player returns the ball from where it came and tries to maintain execution or concentration. The drills show the use of a coach and one player, but they can be done with two players, or with two players and a coach, with the coach acting as a feeder.

Quick Volley Breakdown

(See figure 6-13.)

Objective: To learn not to change the direction of the ball on a stretch-out volley, and to train the hands to be quicker.

Description: The coach (C) stands at the rear corner of the service box, and the player (P) is at the service line. The coach makes shots on both sides low to the player's feet (1-4) to make the player stretch and bend to return the shots. Keep score, and do the drill from the other side of the court.

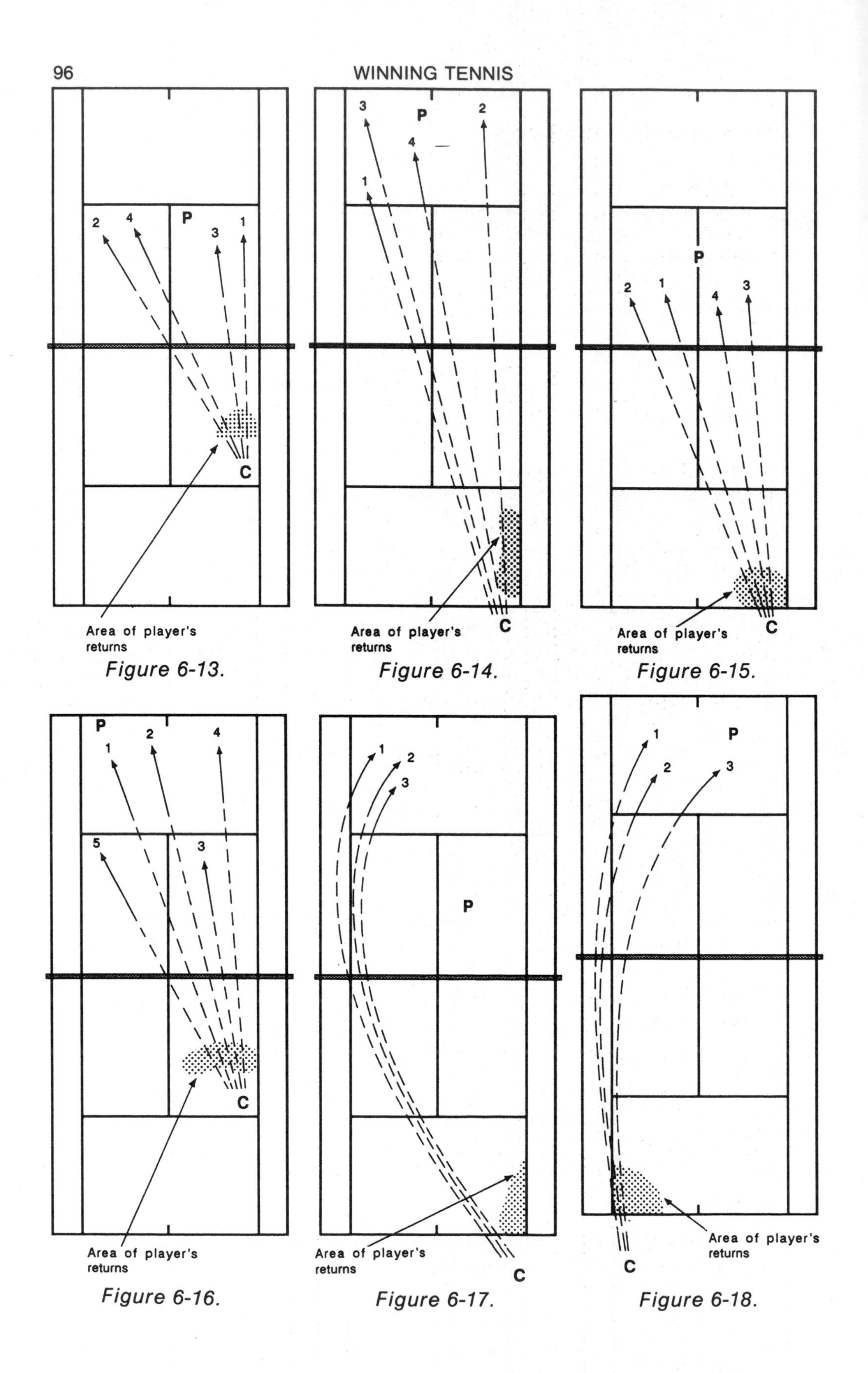

Figure 6-13.

Figure 6-14.

Figure 6-15.

Figure 6-16.

Figure 6-17.

Figure 6-18.

Ground Stroke Breakdown

(See figure 6-14.)

Objective: To learn how to cover the court and make deep shots with no change of direction.

Description: The coach (C) feeds the ball from the corner of the court (1). The player (P) hits the ball back to the coach, and the coach hits each successive shot to a different area of the court (2, 3, and 4). The coach stays in the corner, and the player moves for every ball to any place on the court. The rally continues until either the player or the coach misses. Score should be kept. After the game, the coach should go to the opposite corner and repeat the drill.

Note: If a ball sets up, the player can finish off the shot by returning it to the open court.

Volley Breakdown

(See figure 6-15.)

Objective: To learn to cover the net well and to return all balls without a change of direction to set up the next ball.

Description: The coach (C) feeds a ball (1) from the corner to the player (P), who stands at the net. The player volleys the ball back to the coach, enabling the coach to hit another shot to make the player stretch in another position (2). The coach should mix hard and soft balls as well as wide balls and balls to the middle. Score should be kept, and the drill also should be done to the opposite corner.

Note: If a ball sets up, the player can finish off the shot by returning it to the open court.

Passing Shot Breakdown

(See figure 6-16.)

Objective: To learn how to hit passing shots back from where they came, and to learn which balls to change the direction of and hit to the open court.

Description: The coach (C) stands in the rear corner position of the service box and feeds a ball to the player (P) to begin a rally. The player must hit every shot back to the coach. The coach runs the player to different areas of the court. Score should be kept, and the drill should be done from the opposite short corner.

Note: If an easy ball sets up, the player can finish off the shot by returning it to the open court.

Overhead Breakdown

(See figure 6-17.)

Objective: To learn a consistent and reliable overhead smash.

Description: The coach (C) stands to one side behind the baseline and as close to the fence as possible. The player (P) stands close to the net. The player is forced back with a high defensive lob (1), makes an overhead smash and then tries to close back on the net. The coach then hits another lob (2) and continues (3 and 4) until the player is fatigued. The drill should be repeated with the coach feeding balls to the other side of the court.

Offense-Defense (Weapon)

(See figure 6-18.)

Objective: To turn the player's favorite stroke into a good weapon.

Description: Standing to one side and as far back from the baseline as possible, the coach (C) delivers easy balls to the player's midcourt area (1, 2, and 3). The player (P) moves around the ball and hits the hardest shot possible while still under control, using the favorite stroke, back to the coach. The coach continues to float balls to the player until the player is fatigued. The drill also should be done with the coach feeding balls to the other side of the midcourt.

Two-on-One Drills

Two-on-one drills are used routinely to teach players their limitations on every shot, and they are a great way to learn racquet control and good court movement. Players also must learn to hit balls on the run, and in very different positions. Harry Hopman, the famous Australian Davis Cup Coach, made two-on-one training popular worldwide. He trained his Davis Cup teams and many other international champions in this way.

The player who is being drilled should concentrate on hitting through the two players on the other side of the court, never missing wide, and never missing in the net. The player should concentrate on hitting the ball back from where it came on shots that cannot be controlled or when off-balance. The player can try to change the direction of any ball that pops up to make a penetrating shot. Training in this manner takes on many of the proportions of match play.

Two-on-one training can be performed in four different formations, as follows:

- Two players on the baseline vs. one on the baseline, for ground stroke work.
- Two players at the net vs. one on the baseline, for passing shots and reflex ground strokes.
- Two players on the baseline vs. one at the net, for deep volleys and consistency on volleys.
- Two players at the net vs. one at the net, for quick volleys and reflexes.

These drills can be executed with three players; with three players and a coach, who acts as the feeder; or with two players and a coach.

Two-on-One Baseline Rally

(See figure 6-19.)

Objective: To learn good movement and depth while learning the limitations of each shot and whether or not to change the direction of the ball.

Description: Two players stand at the baseline (Pl and P2), while the third (P3) stands at the opposite baseline. P1 and P2 rally with P3, who covers the entire court.

Two-on-One Passing Shot

(See figure 6-20.)

Objective: To work on movement, quick reflexes, the ability to hit on the run, and deciding whether or not to change the direction of the ball.

Description: Two players (P1 and P2) are at the net, while the third player (P3) stands at the baseline. P1 and P2 hit balls to any spot on P3's side of the court. P3 has to move to each shot and hit back through P1 and P2. P3 quickly learns which balls to change direction and which not to change direction, concentrating on not hitting shots wide or into the net.

Two-on-One Deep Volley

(See figure 6-21.)

Objective: To develop good movement and consistency of volleys.

Description: Two players (P1 and P2) are on the baseline, and the third player (P3) is at the net. P3 returns each shot with a deep volley to either side of the opposite court.

Two-on-One Quick Volley

(See figure 6-22.)

Objective: To improve reflexes and learn limitations in a quick volley situation.

Description: Two players (P1 and P2) stand at the service line and face the third player (P3), who stands at the opposite service line. P1 and P2 hit balls at P3, who returns quick, crisp volleys.

Two-on-One Offense/Defense (Weapon)

(See figure 6-23.)

Objective: To create a good weapon from a player's favorite stroke, and to learn correct footwork when setting up for floating balls.

Description: Two players (P1 and P2) are far behind the baseline, and the third player (P3) is at midcourt on the opposite side. P1 and P2 alternately deliver very soft floating balls to P3 (1-4). P3 moves around each ball and returns it with a favorite stroke, regardless of where it lands. Unlike the one-on-one drill, the player can choose to hit to either corner of the court.

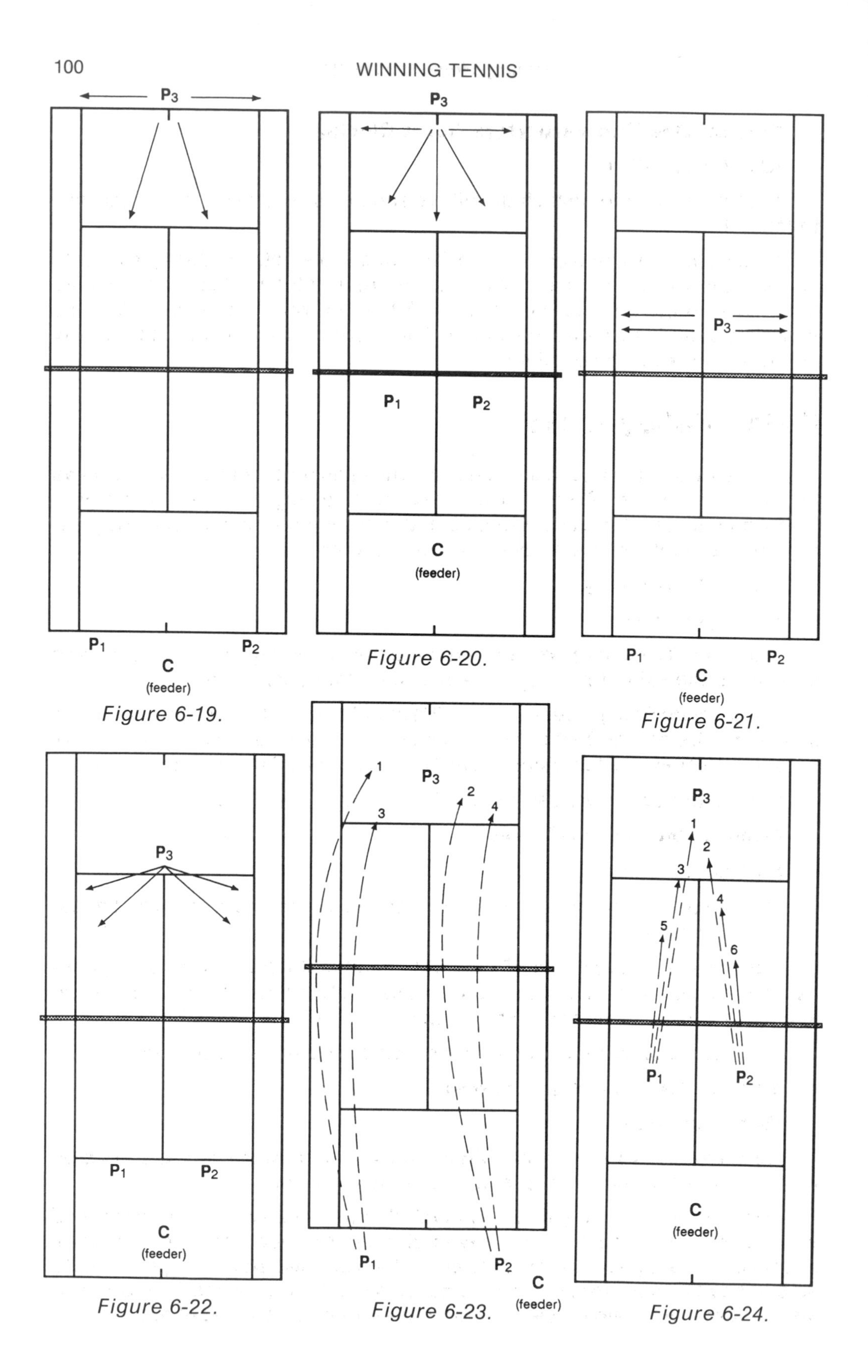

Figure 6-19.

Figure 6-20.

Figure 6-21.

Figure 6-22.

Figure 6-23.

Figure 6-24.

Two-on-One Three-Quarters Court Closing

(See figure 6-24.)

Objective: To learn to hit half-volleys and to make reflex shots on the way to the net.

Description: Two players (P1 and P2) stand at the net. The third player (P3) starts at three-quarters court or toward the rear of the backcourt. P1 and P2 take turns hitting balls at P3's feet as P3 tries to work to the net (1-6). If P3 misses a shot, the drill begins again. A successful drill finds P3 all the way in the net for a finishing volley.

Quick Volley Drills

There's a saying in tennis that quick hands and quick feet make for volleys that are hard to beat. These quick volley drills pay big dividends to a player who wants to develop quick reflexes and control the racquet head. Aggressiveness and intensity are important for these drills.

Shoe Shine Volley

(See figure 6-25.)

Objective: To develop skills in handling the low volley and half-volley and to develop the skill of placing volleys at the other player's feet.

Description: Both players (P1 and P2) stand behind the service line for the entire drill. Using one-half of the singles court as the boundary, each player tries to hit volleys to the other player's shoes. Good footwork is important.

Note: The coach also can feed balls from a side position.

One-on-One Closing Volley

(See figure 6-26.)

Objective: To learn how to close on the net and to develop quick hands, feet, and reflexes.

Description: Both players (Pl and P2) stand in the backcourt. Using one-half of the singles court for the boundary, each player tries to close to the net and win a quick volley point. Score should be kept.

Note: The coach also may start the ball out from a side position.

Two-on-Two Doubles Tracking

(See figure 6-27.)

Objective: To work on quick volleys and to learn how to track as a doubles team. This drill is excellent practice for doubles movement.

Description: Four players (P1 and P2, P3 and P4) start at their respective service lines. The coach feeds balls to different positions, forcing both pairs to shift or slide together in order to cover the returned shots. Players should also attempt to close together on the net as the drill progresses. This drill can also be done with two players on the net and two on the baseline.

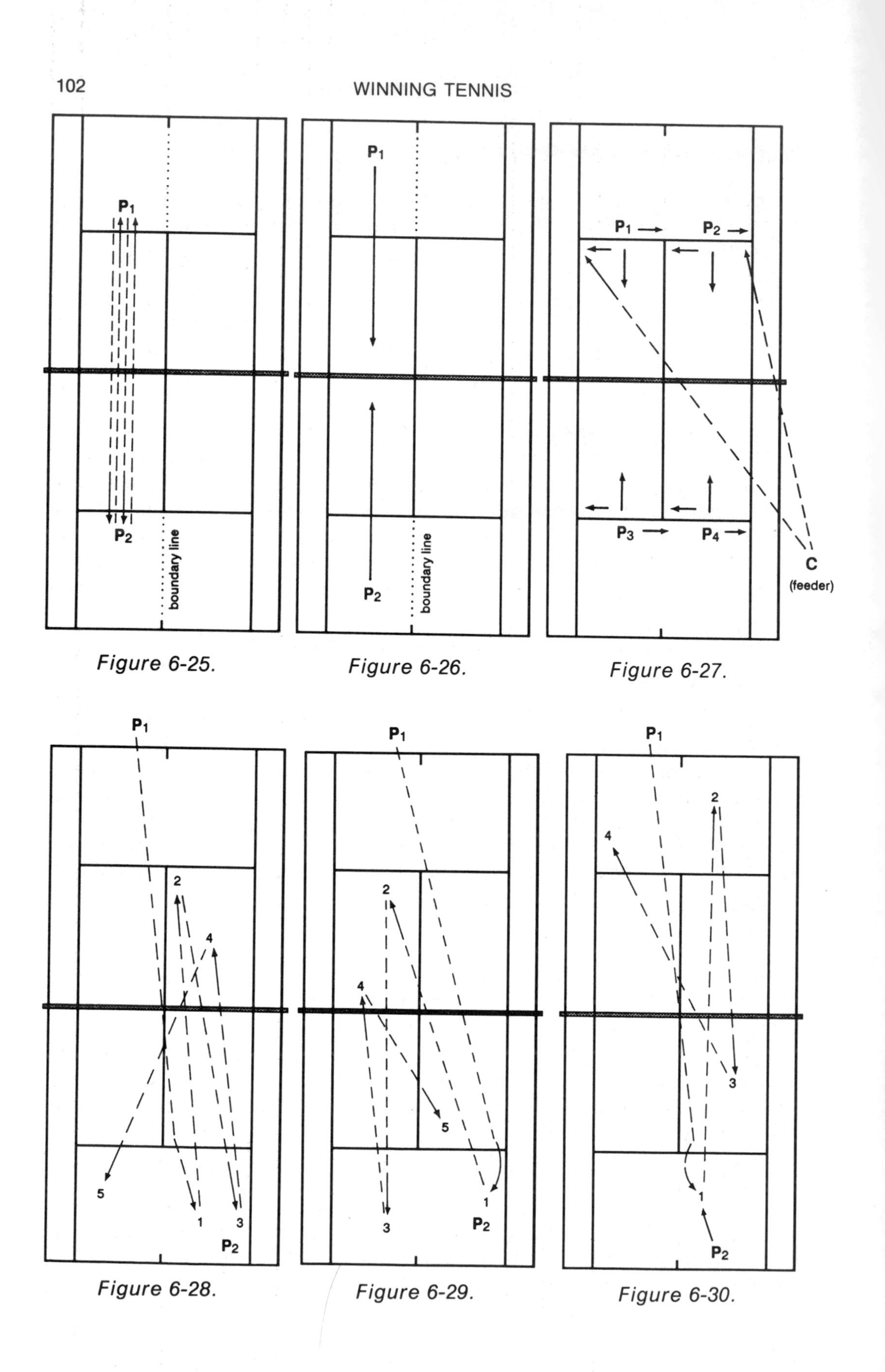

Figure 6-25.

Figure 6-26.

Figure 6-27.

Figure 6-28.

Figure 6-29.

Figure 6-30.

Match Simulation Drills

Certain patterns closely simulate situations that occur again and again during match play. The following drills contain some of these patterns that the player can use to improve skills in playing points in various shot sequences. Although most points cannot be planned from start to finish, the first two or three exchanges usually work well to set up some sequences, and these drills will help the player obtain a good understanding of this concept.

The Serve and Volley-Volley

(See figure 6-28.)

Objective: To work on service placement to the middle of the court, and to work on the first and finishing volleys.

Description: Only one serve is allowed in this drill. The receiver (P2) must return the serve (1) through the middle of the court (2), thereby allowing the server (P1) to make the first volley (3). This first volley should be hit back to where it came from (4), or to the middle of the court. The server then closes off the net and tries to put away the second volley (5). The receiver is allowed to pass on the second ball as well.

The Wide and Glide (Serve Wide and Approach)

(See figure 6-29.)

Objective: To learn how to pull the receiver out of court and then approach the net.

Description: The server (P1) slices the serve wide into the deuce court or kicks the serve wide into the ad court (1). The receiver (P2) returns the ball cross-court (2). The server makes an approach shot off the first return (3) and comes to the net for the finishing volley (4 and 5). The server makes an approach shot off the first return and comes to the net for the finishing volley.

One Serve Receiver Attacks

(See figure 6-30.)

Objective: To put pressure on the server's second serve, to teach the receiver to come to the net on a return of serve, and to work on the server's passing shot under pressure.

Description: The server (P1) is allowed one serve (1). The receiver (P2) must return the serve (2) and come to the net. The server tries to hit a passing shot (3). The receiver now tries to win the point (4) at the net position. Score is kept as in a regular set.

Cross-court Volley with Approach Shot on Short Ball

(See figure 6-31.)

Objective: To learn the importance of cross-court rallies, to learn to keep the court closed, and to learn the skills of making consistent cross-court rallies and down-the-line approach shots.

Description: The two players exchange deep cross-court forehand or backhand shots (1-3) until a short ball is hit (4). This short ball is the cue for the player to make a down-the-line approach shot (5) and to play the point out. Score should be kept.

Cross-court and Down-the-Line Rallies (Control Drill)

(See figure 6-32.)

Objective: To become proficient at changing the direction of the ball during the rally.

Description: One player (P2) rallies from the baseline, directing shots cross-court, and the partner (P1) returns the balls down the line. This forces the players to run from side to side and change the direction of the ball. Score should be kept, and then the drill should be reversed. Players performing this drill should focus on consistency.

Two Volley Passing Shot

(See figure 6-33.)

Objective: To allow one player to work on the approach volley, and to allow another player to work on the first pass and the second passing shot.

Description: One player (P1) starts behind the service line and feeds a ball as an approach shot (1) to the other player (P2), who is on the baseline. P2 must hit the first pass back to P1 (2). Both P1 and P2 then try to win the point (3 and 4). Score should be kept.

Approach-Passing Shot

(See figure 6-34.)

Objective: To work on approach shots and passing shots.

Description: The coach (C) feeds balls from a position to the side and off the court. Two or more players (P1, P2, and P3) line up at the center of the baseline. One player (P4) is on the coach's side of the court at the baseline. The coach feeds a ball into the midcourt (1); each player takes a turn approaching the net with good under-spin approach shots (2), while the player at the baseline tries to make the passing shot (3). Score should be kept.

One-on-One Stretch Pass and Volley

(See figure 6-35.)

Objective: To work on stretching to make down-the-line passing shots and stretch cross-court volleys.

Description: The coach (C) feeds the ball from a position either behind or to the side of the court. The coach hits a ball to the corner of the passing player's (P1) backcourt, forcing the player to stretch for the ball. P1 must make a down-the-line passing shot (2) that the net player (P2) tries to cut off and angle cross-court (3). The coach then hits a wide ball to the passing player's backhand side (4), and the drill is repeated (5 and 6). The passer also may hit the first shot cross-court and then move in to finish the point with the second shot.

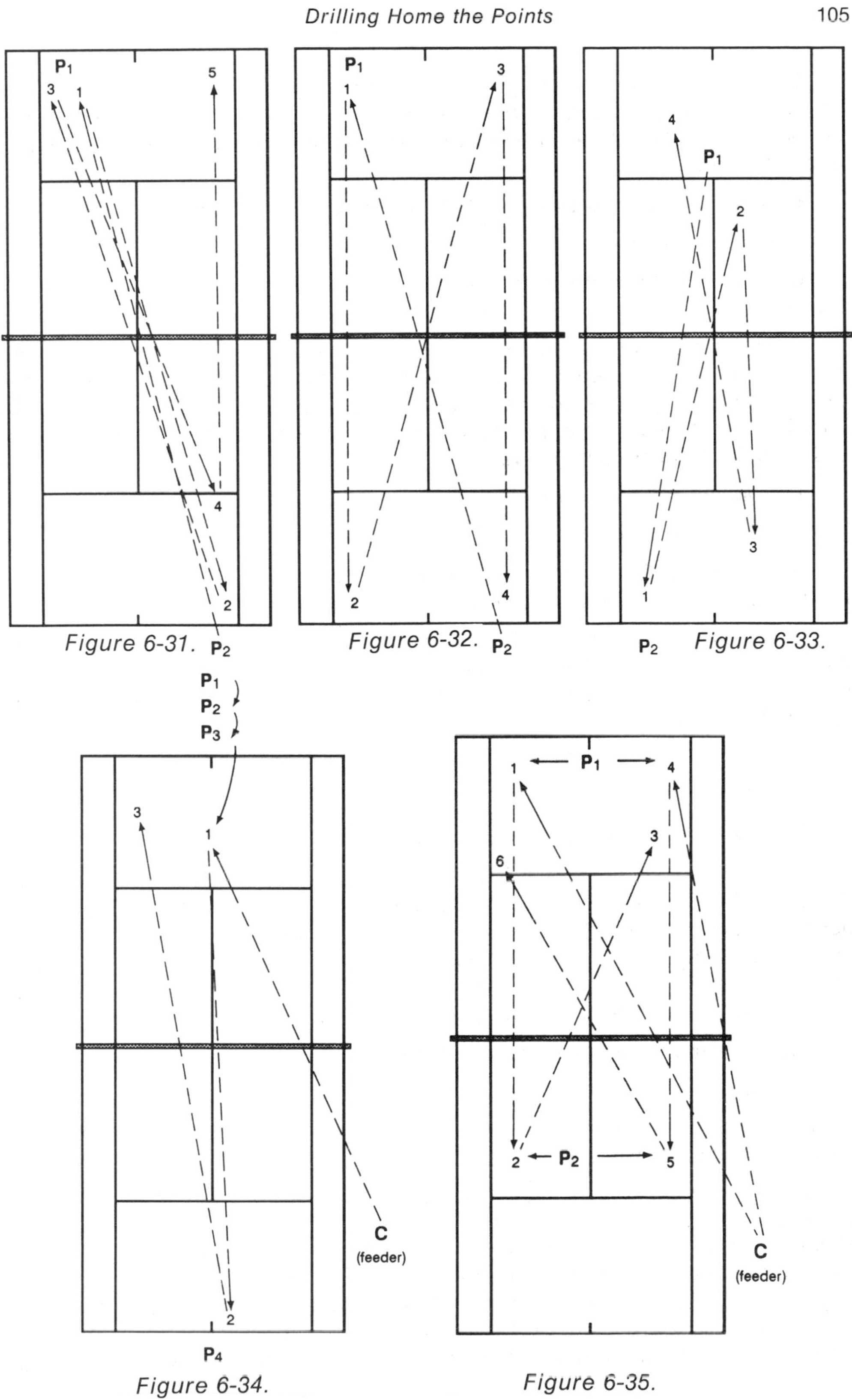

Figure 6-31.

Figure 6-32.

Figure 6-33.

Figure 6-34.

Figure 6-35.

Serving Drills

Wrist Serving

Objective: To develop a quicker wrist snap for better racquet head speed on the serve.

Description: The server stands with the side of the body facing the net and both feet placed firmly on the ground. As the toss is delivered, the server's body is frozen in this sideways position, and the only power used for the stroke comes from the snap of the wrist. It is very important that the feet, legs, hips, upper body, and head all stay sideways so that the wrist action is the predominant power source. The arm, wrist, and racquet head should become one and move like a whip with the racquet head cracking through the ball. The server should serve 50 to 75 balls before regular practice of the serve.

Placement Cues

Objective: To give the player a very basic concept of placement and accuracy.

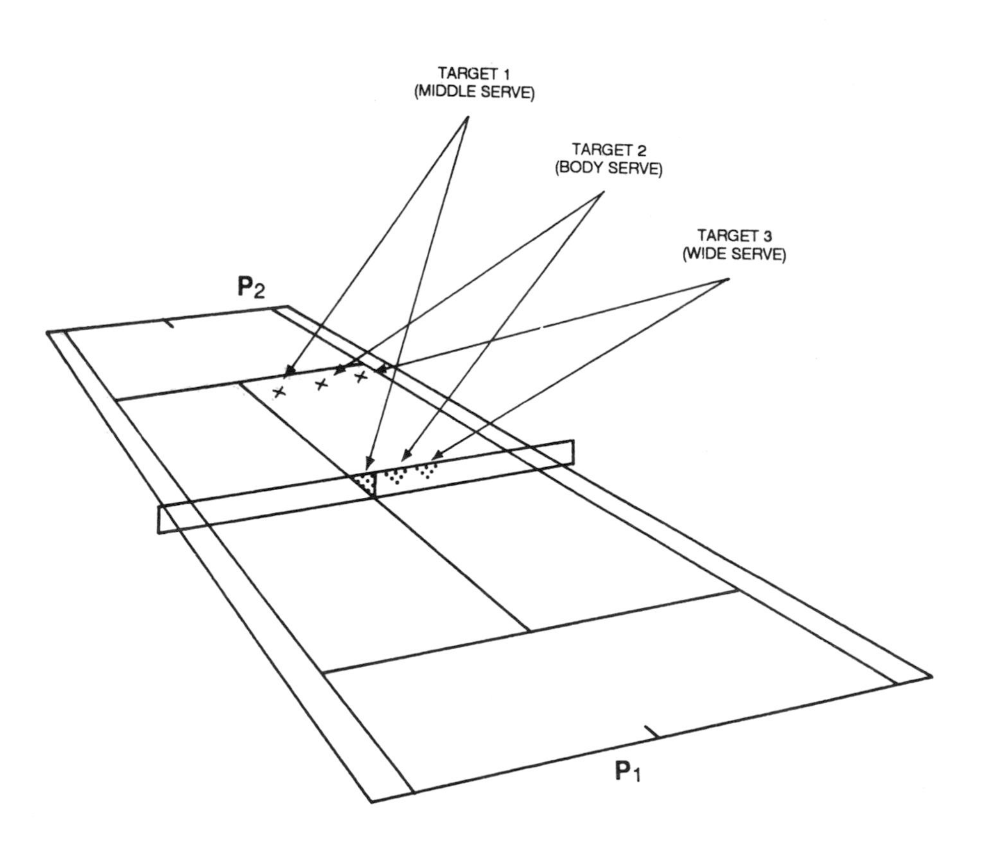

Figure 6-36.

Description: Just as a bowler looks at the arrows on the lane, and just as a hunter looks through the sight on a gun, a server can look at an area of the net as a directional target for better service accuracy. A player can improve the placement of middle line serves by standing in the ready position and using the V-shaped area formed by the center strap and the opponent's center service line to direct a serve to Target 1. The server can direct a body serve to Target 2 by aligning the opponent's feet with a corresponding spot at the top of the net. A wide corner serve to Target 3 can be directed by lining up part of the net with the target. Figure 6-36 illustrates serves to the deuce court; these targets also can be used when serving to the ad court.

Simulate Set Play for Practice Situations

Many times the rules of tennis can be altered to emphasize specific skills during practice. Not only does this offer a change of pace that can be fun for players, it enables them to focus on specific aspects of their games or on situations that might come up in a match. Some examples follow:

- Play a set, scoring on the service game only, as in volleyball and racquetball. This emphasizes learning how to hold serve.
- Play a set scoring on the return game only. This emphasizes learning how to break serve.
- Play sets in which the server is allowed only one serve, and the receiver must come to the net. This teaches a good second serve as well as coming to the net on a return, and helps develop passing shots.
- Play a set in which you must hold serve before you turn it over to the opponent. In the first service game, the score starts at 0-40; the second service game starts at 0-30, the third game at 0-15, then 0-0 — as long as it takes to hold serve. This teaches the server how to come from behind on the service game, and teaches the receiver to take advantage of early opportunities. This concept works well for doubles as well.
- Play a set serving only to the deuce court or only to the ad court, for the entire set. This gives the server a chance to groove the serve and to learn what the options and plays are to run in each court.
- Play sets starting at deuce in every game. This system allows multi-sets or competitions to be played in a short time while placing emphasis on the very critical part of each game.
- Play sets allowing only one serve.
- Play sets allowing only serve and volley, or allowing no net play.
- Play sets in which both players stand inside the baseline for all shots. This teaches taking balls on the rise and dealing with odd bounces.
- Play conversion sets (three points in a row). A game can only be won if three consecutive points are won by a player.

Bjorn Borg had a flair for playing hard, and winning with class.

"Class never runs scared;
it is surefooted and confident.
Class never makes excuses;
it takes its lumps and learns from past mistakes.
Class is real. You can't fake it."

—Unknown

7

Harnessing the Stallion

No one enjoys losing, whether it's in a social game or the Wimbledon finals. There's a loser for every winner in most forms of competition, however, and many times the outcome is determined by a competitor's mental approach. That's why it's important to determine just how seriously you want to take the game before you can achieve maximum enjoyment from it.

"Social competitors" play only occasionally, and usually with friends. Although everyone usually gives their best effort, winning and losing are taken in stride and everyone in the group understands that the main objective is to release energy and have fun.

The "weekend warrior" emerges when middle age strikes the body of the competitive athlete, but the mind and spirit won't let go of youth. Many of these players take tennis as seriously as ever, and believe they are close to taking their game to another level. They are constantly looking for ways to improve, but job, family and other commitments take up a large part of their time. This can result in frustration if unrealistic expectations are not met. Be ready for a battle when you're on the court against this opponent.

Many other players, however, compete as hard as they can every time on the court, but keep winning and losing in perspective. If a realistic approach is taken toward expectations, it can be fun to compete with the weekend warrior. The proper attitude is a necessity for maximum enjoyment.

As players improve, they usually want to compete, whether it be at the club level, the high school level or in sanctioned tournament events. Regardless, players should give their best efforts — mentally, physically and emotionally — toward winning, and that's what this chapter is about.

Understanding the Emotions of Competition

Competition makes something in all of us surface that we have trouble understanding or controlling.

"I'm just not a competitive person," the young girl said to her parents as she cried and walked away from the tennis court after losing her first match. "When the score got close, I got a big lump in my throat, and I felt like I might be sick to my stomach. My legs got weak and I felt like just not trying any more."

Meanwhile, the girl's friend on the other side of the net was talking with her parents. "It was nice to win, but I felt bad for Jane. She seemed so afraid and nervous; I hope it doesn't hurt our friendship. But WOW! It was so exciting to compete today. I had so much positive energy, I felt I could run all day!"

Regardless of what our standards may be as to how a person should feel and behave during competition, the fact remains that each individual reacts to a competitive situation differently. Some are drawn to it, even inspired by it, while others fear it. Psychologists call it the fight-or-flight syndrome. However, this is something that can be developed until the right perspective is achieved.

Set Goals, Train Hard, Play Fair

Being competitive while playing fair and having fun should be the goal of all of us.

Tennis is an individual sport, and therefore exposes more of our inner feelings and emotions than a team sport would. Winning and losing are basically ours to achieve, and neither the credit nor the blame can be passed to teammates.

One of the great benefits of playing individual sports is that they help you to learn about yourself and what happens to your personality under pressure. I have a framed quote on my office wall that says, "Tennis undresses you like no other sport, sometimes even down to the soul. It is so important to train our fundamentals well so that even in the nakedness of adversity, our substance will endure and prevail."

Through competition, we sometimes like what we find out about ourselves and sometimes don't. The important thing is that we learn, so we can grow in a way that enables us to express ourselves competitively in an acceptable fashion.

Athletics is one of the most pure and basic forms of expression. Much like art to the artist and music to the musician, the competitive arena allows the athlete one of the few forums where the inner self can be unleashed for a short period of freedom. Finding the balance between unleashed competitiveness and emotional restraint is the primary goal in becoming a fair but tough competitor.

Corralling the Stallion

Coaching Greg, my senior captain and leader, was one of the most interesting and challenging experiences I've ever had. His disposition and nature away from the tennis court was one of feeling, gentleness, and a very touching warmth that showed a true depth of character.

During competitive situations, however, his moods and actions sometimes shifted dramatically from out-of-control anger to a near total withdrawal of energy. He occasionally had moments of brilliance, when everything came together for him. This "zone" was what we sought for him throughout his career. Because of his sensitive nature, the fierce, competitive image seemed unnatural for him, but it often came out when under attack by his opponent.

The breakthrough that led to finding a proper balance and perspective for him was an observation given by an assistant coach.

"Greg, he said, "with all of his sensitive and calm-hearted tendencies, has a stallion inside of him that is fighting to come out. Greg's calm nature is afraid of the stallion that might run wild all over what he wants to accomplish.

"The key for him is to ride that stallion and use his wonderful inner nature to control its reins so that its strength and energy can be channeled properly into his competitive situations."

This perspective gave Greg an excellent understanding of how to tap his competitiveness in a useful manner, giving him greater inner peace when competing. When the athlete finds this balance, maximum potential can be achieved

The Fight or Flight Syndrome

Robert, a sophomore, was one of my most talented athletes, but also one of the most undisciplined. He had never made a commitment to being his best, because in high school he was able to succeed without really trying. College was a different matter, because everyone around him was just as talented as him. Robert began losing frequently, and it was a painful experience.

I kept telling him that he was going to be successful only if he made a complete commitment to improving his game, and made it quickly. The losses were painful enough that Robert made the commitment, and for six weeks his workouts were exceptional. He gave 100 percent effort in all that he did.

My anticipation was high as our next major tournament arrived. But when the match started, I couldn't believe my eyes. This same player who had worked and trained for six weeks was "tanking" (giving up) in his first match.

"Why, why, why?" I asked him, "after so much hard work would you just give up?" He replied that he didn't really know why, except that at the moment of battle he became terribly afraid and withdrew energy.

Some refer to it as the "fight or flight" syndrome. Under the stress of a competitive situation, some people rise to the occasion, while others retreat. This is especially true when a great commitment has been made to the activity and the person cares a great deal.

After the tournament, I drew up the following diagram to help explain that his reaction was quite normal, but that it was important for him to go to the next step.

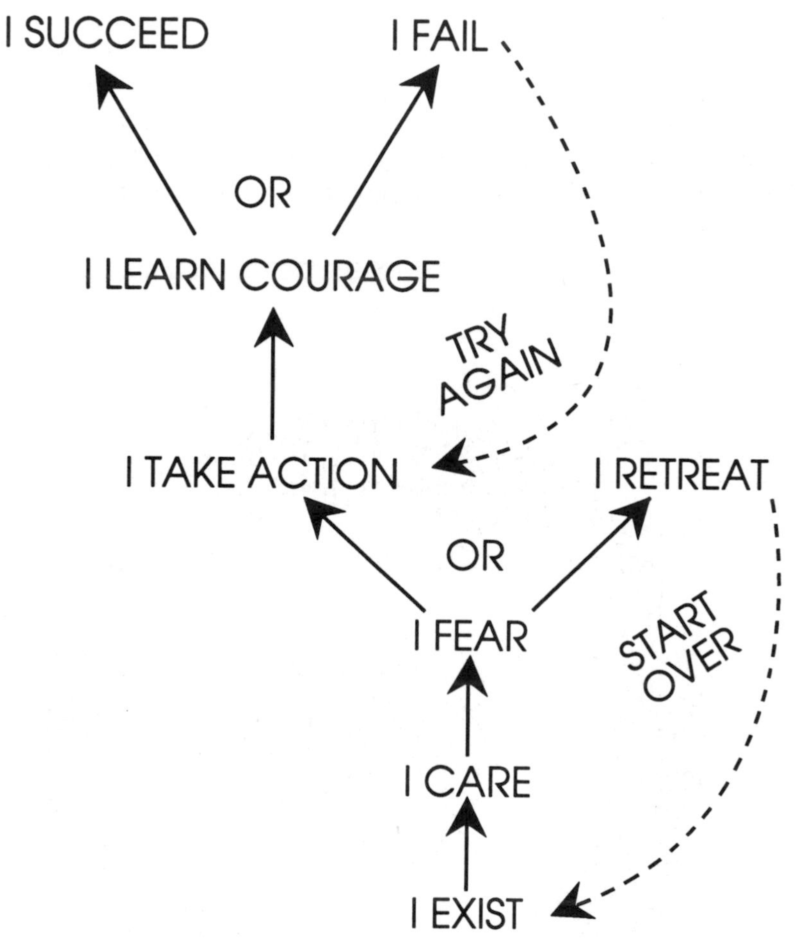

Figure 7-1. Arriving at the point of commitment.

If you don't care you are taking no risks, and therefore have no fear. The biggest job initially is to bring yourself to the point of commitment and then work through the fear.

Finding "the Zone"

One of the best clutch competitors I've ever coached was Kent Kinnear. Kent seemed to pull out close match after close match during his career. It truly was never over until it was over when you played him. He always seemed to have that sense of calm under pressure that is so hard to teach athletes. An opposing coach once remarked, "You can sometimes beat Kent's game, but you can never beat Kent."

Kent had a way of finding that elusive balance of taking what he did seriously, but never taking himself too seriously. His maturity in competitive situations seemed to stem from a very solid inner peace, and was a tremendous example to all around him.

One of the best recipes I have seen for tennis players trying to find that balance is by sports psychologist Jim Loehr in his book and video, *Mental Toughness*. His theory, shown in the following diagram, is a very simple formula that helps find that perfect emotional playing "zone" for competition. This tool is one of the most practical I have found to use with competitive players.

Figure 7-2. Jim Loehr's mental toughness target.

Loehr describes four emotional responses that occur under the pressure of competitive situations by the rings on a target.

The outer ring, furthest from the bull's eye, shows giving up, or "tanking." This is the first response many people make under pressure. They tell themselves it is just not worth it to give 100 percent of their effort. This response seems to protect the ego, but it never leads to good results in the long run.

The next ring of the target is the anger zone. Many people wind up here during competitive situations. This is a little better than tanking, because you don't completely give up, but it is still quite non-productive. Although it feels good for a moment to lose your temper, good performance rarely results from anger, and your reputation as a sportsman may be damaged as well.

The third ring shows "choking." This is one of the most feared responses for an athlete. To be a choker carries a stigma that is difficult to overcome. However, becoming nervous and unsure of oneself under pressure is not only better than tanking and anger, it usually is the journey the athlete must endure en route to being a good competitor. It means the athletes cares a lot, but hasn't yet learned how to transfer that caring into motor skills. That process takes time for the best of athletes, and is neither an overnight nor an effortless process.

Choking is much better than tanking or anger, and should be recognized as such. An athlete who chokes is only one step away from the very best response in a competitive situation: the *challenge response*.

Here, all of the athlete's energy is focused. The body, mind, and emotions all work as one unit, striving for the same objective. The athlete feels alert, energized and confident, and is able to perform at the peak level. Athletes who experience this "challenge zone" understand the ultimate feeling of competition — a total-release performance without the conflict of emotions that are common under fire.

This target can help athletes bring their best performance from the depths of their souls to the playing field. It is a great guideline for finding that perfect balance of corralling and riding the stallion within.

In finding your competitive demeanor, it is important to realize that you have a unique disposition that cannot and should not be changed. As a coach, I believe that attitude can be changed, but our innate disposition is the framework we have to work from.

Beginning players, when they are struggling for confidence, should remember that they are the No. 1 player in the world at their style of play. Believe in it.

"Insist on yourself, never imitate.
That which each can do best,
none but his maker can teach."

—Ralph Waldo Emerson

8

Selecting a Playing Style

One of the most important decisions a player must make is choosing the style that best suits his or her ability and temperament. Lessons and coaching can dramatically speed the development of a player's technical skills, but it is critical that good judgment be used in developing a game that fits an individual physically, mentally, and emotionally. This can save months or even years in development.

Very few people are gifted enough to do everything well, and it is important to understand one's own strengths so that they can be used to their fullest. It is crucial to understand, however, that style must coincide with temperament.

Bjorn Borg's very disciplined and methodical style would not have been successful if his temperament had been like that of Illie Nastase. Likewise, Nastase's flashy, aggressive game probably would not have been successful with Borg's even temperament. Nastase, McEnroe, and Laver all were creative learners. They all were champions, and they all were successful within their styles and their mental and emotional framework. Borg, Wilander, and Rosewall all were seemingly repetitive learners, successful in their own way and special because of their unique makeup.

Players eventually develop styles that reflect their own personalities. Anyone who attempts to adapt to a playing style that does not fit his or her personality will not enjoy the game as much.

All players should learn the physical skills of stroke technique, but they can concentrate on one of three game styles: the counter- punching game, the attacking game, or the all-court game.

Be Yourself

Over the Christmas holidays in 1983, my team was participating in an indoor tournament in New Orleans. The tournament was to feature a match-up between two of the top collegiate players in the country, each of whom had sharply different styles of play. One was an aggressive serve-and-volley player, and the other was the No. 2-ranked player in the United States, Johnny Levine from the University of Texas.

At first, the match reminded me of some of the exciting Wimbledon matches between McEnroe and Borg in the early 1980s. As the match progressed, however, it quickly became disappointing. Levine won in 35 minutes, 6-1, 6-0. I wondered how a match with such great possibilities could end with such a lopsided score. The reaction of my players and many other bystanders was that Levine was a great player who was very physically and mentally tough and would make a great pro. I was disappointed by this simple reasoning.

Levine's opponent walked up to the lounge area with the rest of the players, and his reaction was pretty much the same as those who watched the match. "I don't really know what happened," he said. "I tried everything, and nothing worked."

After he said this, I turned to my players and asked, "Who in the world is good at everything?" I told them that I would have rather heard him say, "I played my game. He was just better at his style than I was at my style."

Some players, when their confidence cracks during a match, revert to another style of play. As soon as this happens, the match is pretty much over. Players are never as good at other styles as they are at their own. An old rule of tennis is that you always make changes in a losing game, but not in a winning game. This can be somewhat misleading. What this reallly means is that you make adjustments to your style, not change your style. I always tell my players, "You are No. 1 in the world at the way you play. The best you can ever be at someone else's style is No. 2."

You're usually just grasping at straws when you try a lot of different styles. This does not mean you cannot make adjustments in playing different strategies within your style, but the strategy should always be to stick to the style that is most familiar to you. To try many different options usually only makes it easier for your opponent and further confuses you.

The Counter-Punching Game

The counter-punching style favors athletes who are relaxed and nonconfrontational by nature, but are tough-minded. The primary skills to learn are good passing shots and lobbing, a good return of serve, and good side-to-side movement on the baseline. Consistency, placement, and depth of shots should be areas of concern during practice sessions.

The advantage of the counter-punch game is that it is the easiest style to learn, and it gives the fastest results. A player has fewer decisions to make than with another style, because this style relies on reacting and countering rather than dictating the points with aggressive play.

An adept counter-puncher can usually defeat an intermediate player, but problems arise when facing a skilled aggressive player or another counter-puncher who is slightly better. This is the best style of play, however, for smaller players, or those who rely on speed. Borg and Michael Chang are probably two of the best counter-punchers in the history of tennis.

The Attacking Game

The attacking game style is suited to a good athlete with an aggressive temperament, or an athlete of large physical stature who has a nonaggressive temperament (such as Stan Smith) but doesn't make unforced errors.

The net rusher

The skills needed for this style of play include a strong serve, good approach shots, consistent first volleys, and a good overhead smash. Errors will be made with an attacking style, but the athlete should always remember to make them aggressively and decisively. Doubt and hesitation are the culprits for the attacking player, so controlled aggression is critical. Taking care of details is critical, as is taking time between points and being fully aware of momentum swings. John McEnroe and Stefan Edberg are examples of great net-rushers.

The attacking baseliner

An attacking game also can be played from the baseline, but a high level of confidence in one's ground strokes is critical. Excellent control of the spin shots is needed so that adjustments can be made in adverse situations where timing may be thrown off, such as by the wind or an opponent's strange style.

The attacking baseliner takes greater risks than most players from the baseline, but does not give the opponent a quick target like a net rusher does. The attacking baseliner, therefore, can deliver a blow without taking the chance of being passed at the net. Andre Agassi, Jim Courier and Monica Seles all are good examples of attacking baseliners.

All the attacking styles take longer to develop, but can give the player opportunities for big wins. Players who devote themselves to an attacking game will be less consistent at first, and must be patient with themselves even while taking some losses along the way.

The All-Court Game

The all-court game is the best style to teach if there is adequate time to train and if the athlete is versatile and well-equipped physically, mentally, and emotionally. All the skills that enable the counter-puncher and the attacking player to be successful are needed to play the all-court game, so this style takes the longest time to learn and requires the most patience.

Consistency, placement, depth, spin, and power are needed with all the strokes, so the player must have a disciplined temperament and be prepared for occasional poor performances. It also is critical to master momentum control and understand the flow of the match. Still, mastering this style produces the best results of any style of play.

The following chart shows the skills needed for building a particular style. Once again, the style used needs to be in balance with the player's unique temperament and personality.

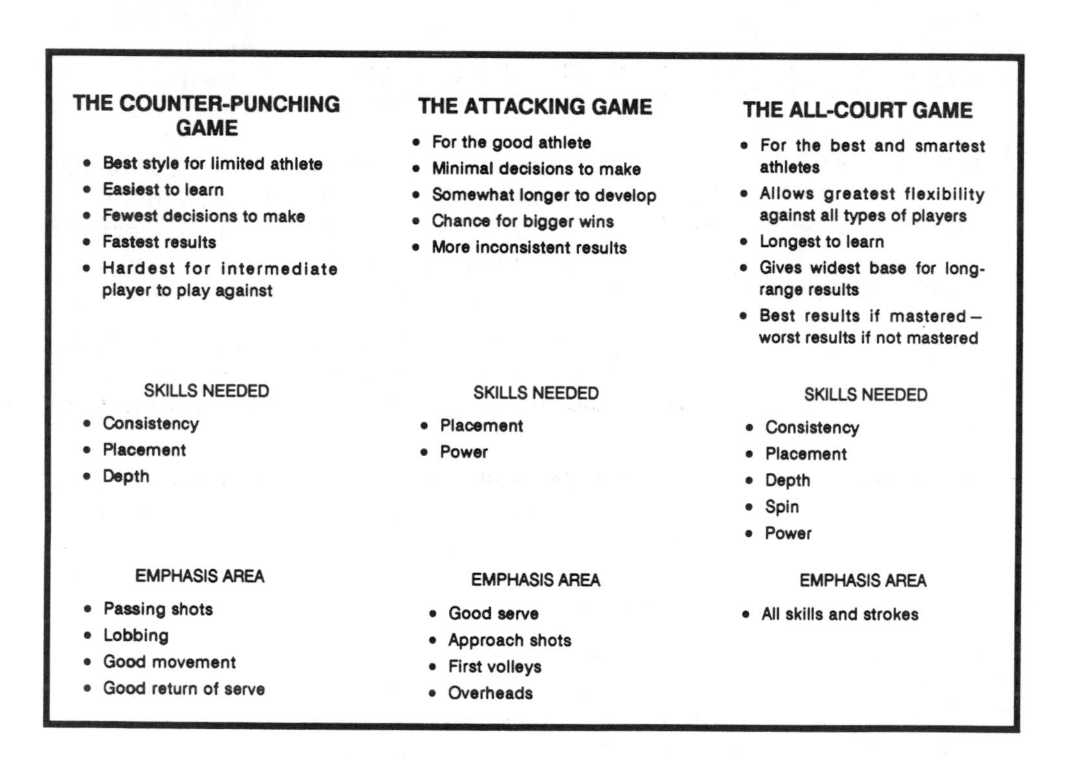

Figure 8-1. Building your best game.

*"Let our advance worrying
become advance thinking and planning."*

— Winston Churchill

9

Preparing to Play

Much of a tennis player's success starts with good pre-match preparation. A player's scope of the "pre-match" period, however, should be widened to include the day before a match, if not more. Tennis is an individual sport and many of the variables leading up to the start of a match can be controlled, therefore consistent routines for pre-match preparation should be developed.

Whatever the routine, it should fit the style and personality of the player. A team routine is much the same. It should fit the image and personality of the team, and the guidelines should be consistent in order to gain the trust and confidence of team members.

The body, the mind, and the emotions should all be prepared for a match: the body should be warmed up, strategy should be reviewed, and attention should be given to emotional balance. On the day prior to competition, special attention should be paid to diet and rest. Strenuous workouts should not be conducted within 48 hours of the match.

A routine for a team the day of the match might be to meet at the match site an hour before the start of the match. A 30-minute warm-up period is optimal. The next 15 minutes should be spent in a brief strategy session on what to expect from the match and the course of action to use against the opponent. The last few moments before the match should be spent in preparing the emotions for the battle ahead.

Physical, Mental, and Emotional Preparation

The following checklist contains the important physical, mental, and emotional considerations to review before the match starts. It starts with the more fundamental and obvious, and progresses to greater detail.

- Follow a consistent routine before the match.
- Be comfortable with a consistent routine that will be used during the match between points that have been won or lost.
- Take care of all physical details:
    a. Eat right.
    b. Get enough sleep.
    c. Have the right equipment.
    d. Perform an adequate warm-up and stretching routine.

Understand your game plan

Understanding the playing styles of different players and how they affect your performance is one of the most confusing aspects of planning strategies for a match. Knowing exactly what to do in all situations is nearly impossible; thus, it is critical for the player to have a set routine to follow in various recognizable situations.

The two defining factors in a match are, obviously, your play and your opponent's play. The relationship between these factors can be explained by a simple formula:

My winners minus *my errors* must be greater than my *opponent's winners* minus my *opponent's errors*. Simplified, it reads as follows:

$$MW - ME > OW - OE$$

The applications of this formula are many, but it should be remembered that seldom can more than 50 percent of the outcome of a match be controlled. Only the most advanced players are able to force opponents to play poorly. Therefore, the first priority in a player's strategy should be to control his or her own 50 percent that can be controlled.

The confidence players have in their own tools eventually will be the factor that dents the confidence of their opponents. If players cannot trust in their style of play and maintain their style throughout a match, all other strategies are worthless.

This does not mean players should be bullheaded and play only one way, never making adjustments. It means players should control how they want to play, forcing opponents to react. Winners act, losers react.

Coping with different styles

What adjustments should be made when you are playing someone with a different game style?

The combinations of styles are endless, but having a procedure can be helpful in planning strategy against a player with a different style than your own. The best way to do this is to use the return game to bring the opponent out of his or her favorite style.

If you are playing against a powerful server, for example, you would want to force the player away from a serve-and-volley style by coming to the net as often as possible on your returns. This may keep the opponent from attacking the net at critical times. Or, you would make a baseline player play long and tedious games when that player is serving. This might cause the player to become frustrated and rush to the net to try to finish points faster.

The rule is: *On my serve I play like me, on the opponent's serve I play like my opponent.*

Most players either play their service game or their return game very naturally, but struggle with the other. You should be more structured and prepared on what you'd like to do with the one that you find more awkward.

Playing against a similar style

It was always amazing to see Bjorn Borg beat Guillermo Vilas so badly in almost all of their meetings, although both were great players with seemingly identical styles. Because of the scoring system used in tennis, however, if two players have nearly identical styles of play, it takes only a slight edge, perhaps only one or two percent more proficiency, for a player to win by lopsided scores.

When playing styles are alike, the lesser player has no way to attack the superior player, and will almost always lose. For years, Chris Evert won match after match against baseline players just slightly less adept than she. Her biggest threats were players like Evonne Goolagong, Martina Navratilova, and Hana Mandlikova, all of whom played contrasting styles.

In playing a match against an opponent with the same style, you have two alternatives: you can stick with your style, or you can play another style. If you are favored, the choice is obvious. If you are the lesser player, abandoning your style violates the first law of strategy: *trust your game*.

The best choice is to be hardheaded and stick with your game, remembering that although you may have a hard time hurting your opponent, your opponent also might have a hard time hurting you, and the difference between winning and losing might be only one percent. You might have opportunities to attack in a different manner effectively, but remember to stay with your style, for that is what you are best at.

Evaluate the Situation and Deal with it

What is the situation? How might my opponent play? What should I expect? Can I handle it? Am I ready for a tough match?

These are all questions that are certainly worth asking before taking the court against any opponent. Different situations present different challenges. A huge mistake that coaches and athletes make is to either avoid their roles as they enter competition or to think that one situation is the same as all others.

Players tend to begin playing without evaluating the situation, because of their doubts and anxieties, inexperience, or perhaps procrastination. The problem is that what happens in a match may be totally different than what the player expects. This places a player in the role of the reactor in a competitive situation.

Ironically, many great players prove to be excellent crisis managers, but this is not a good approach because it is not reliable. It is better to recognize and prepare for the job at hand.

Match roles

Players carry specific roles into a match. When you do not know your opponent, you assume one of the following roles:

The favorite. Being favored is an advantage that can cause your opponent to play tentatively or crack under pressure, but you still must be prepared for a tough match. Your opponent might figure he or she has nothing to lose and play loose and fearlessly.

The underdog. The opponent's reputation might be greater than is deserved. It's important to trust your own game from start to finish. Remember, your regular stuff is good enough.

Neither favorite nor underdog. This is the easiest role in which to enter a match, because you can do so without preconceptions. You can play your own game, and respect your opponent's. The outcome will be decided by who believes in and executes the game plan best at critical times.

When you know your opponent, you will find yourself in one of the following situations:

You have played the opponent and won. This gives you a definite emotional advantage. If you concentrate and work hard early in the match to prevent the opponent from gaining confidence, you should win comfortably.

You have played the opponent and lost. This match must be played with a great deal of enthusiasm and outward confidence. It is one of the hardest to turn into victory because of the established pecking order, but the opponent might be overconfident and not play as hard.

You have never played the opponent. If this is the case, either:

a. *You are favored.* Show plenlty of outer confidence and work hard early in the match. Your reputation gives you a definite advantage if you show no weakness of attitude.

b. *The opponent is favored.* The mystique of your favored opponent must be challenged. Play with enthusiasm and trust your game totally.

c. *It is an even match-up.* This will start as a very nervous match. There are no pre-match conceptions, but lack of a track record against this opponent makes it critical to trust your game from start to finish and to show respect for your opponent.

Realize that each of these situations presents a different challenge for which you must be ready. Each challenge may not be comfortable to you emotionally. The best way to approach each one is to acknowledge the pressure and attack it head-on.

Pressure and Peak Performance

To understand inconsistency in performance, one should understand pressure and how it relates to achieving peak performance.

The proper level of stress and the athlete's ability to manage the pressure caused by stress are critical to optimal performance. A balance must be maintained throughout the match. Being ahead tends to make a player relax, and being behind tends to put pressure on a player. Maintaining a balance requires an understanding of the benefits of pressure on performance.

As the stress curve in figure 9-1 illustrates, a medial amount of pressure produces the best performance.

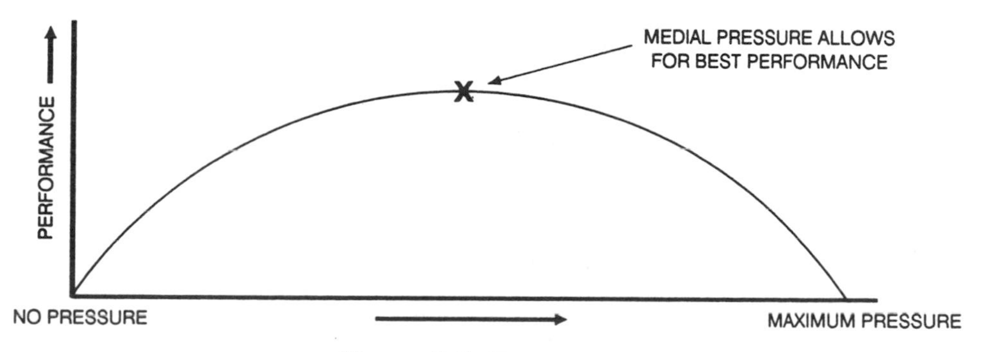

Figure 9-1. Pressure curve.

The balance of pressure

As a player, you should try to recognize when you are feeling too much or too little pressure during performance. Over time, coaches must learn to help each player feel the right balance of pressure. Pre-match preparation has a lot to do with finding this balance of pressure, but adjustments can be made even after the match starts.

Although better players tend to raise their levels of play when they are behind, many players begin to press when they are behind, even if only by a point. Good players usually do not make bad mistakes when they are behind unless they are cracking.

Your first bad mistake or unforced error while trailing in a match should draw your immediate attention, because this is almost always an indication that you are either pressing or have lost confidence. It usually is easy to recognize when a player is trying too hard, because the player will be rushing and appear frantic. At this stage, it is critical to try to relax.

Players who are leading in a match, however, often relax too much and make careless errors. The following statement summarizes match flow: "When players are behind, they make their best shots; when they are ahead, they become careless."

Respect Your Opponent

A balance of respect is the key to consistent performance. It is a mistake for any athlete to get too cocky, but lack of confidence is just as harmful. The correct balance of respect for yourself and your opponent is critical for optimal performance. Confidence? Cockiness? Humility? Which is best?

I teach my players the following definitions:

> *Confidence — belief in self plus respect for opponent*
>
> *Cockiness — belief in self minus respect for opponent*

Confidence is always better than cockiness in a competitive situation. The former gets the job done, the latter sets you up for a big fall.

Four things can happen during a point to cause a possible reaction or mood swing: 1) you can make an error, 2) you can make a good shot, 3) your opponent can make an error, or 4) your opponent can make a good shot. A player's reaction to each of these depends largely on attitude.

Participants in individual sports often do not like to acknowledge the strengths or accomplishments of another competitor. They believe that doing so lessens their own stature or confidence.

Actually, the opposite is true. It is the confident athlete who can give credit to another athlete and separate performance from feelings. Not having respect for an opponent is one of the easiest traps to fall into, though. Players tend to save their greatest concentration and energy for what they perceive as their toughest battles.

The possible reactions to the four scenarios are shown in figures 9-2 and 9-3. If you lack respect for your opponent, you are unlikely to perform at or near your peak level, no matter who you are playing.

You might be able to react positively when bad things happen while playing an opponent you do not respect, but rarely does anything good come from this attitude. By lacking respect for your opponent, you put yourself in a no-win situation. Having something to gain is a key ingredient to motivating yourself for a good performance, and respect for your opponent is critical to having something to gain.

Having too much respect for your opponent, however, can present other problems. Perhaps your opponent beat you last time, or you hold the opponent somewhat in awe. Because of the pecking order in tennis, all players are initially in an underdog role. You almost always have to lose before you can win. The transition from being the underdog to becoming the favored player is a tough one, and this growth usually occurs in cycles. It is extremely difficult to win in the underdog role, especially if you have too much respect for your opponent.

The lack of confidence that generally accompanies being an underdog contributes to erratic play in a match, which further erodes confidence. It can be difficult to break this cycle and maintain a balanced outlook.

The underdog role can be a fun one if you have the proper mental outlook. Expectations tend to be low for you, but you must guard against sharing those expectations so that you don't eventually live down to them. You might dictate the tempo of the match for long periods and play with authority, but at critical stages the favored opponent will take charge if you succumb to the expectations of your role. Remember, winners act and losers react.

To maintain the proper outlook going into a match, you should keep reminding yourself, "I know I can win, but I know my opponent can win too if I'm not at my best." This attitude puts the athlete in a state of absolute readiness for a tough battle.

Many athletes reject this attitude, because giving the opponent respect and recognizing the difficulty of the challenge supposedly places them in a vulnerable position. Acknowledging this vulnerability can make them uneasy, but it should help prepare them mentally and emotionally.

If you have the proper balance of respect for your opponent, your reactions to your good and bad shots and your opponent's good and bad shots will be more consistent, and lead to a better and more consistent performance, as shown in figure 9-3.

The smart and experienced competitor is always aware that emotional balance is critical for good play. The foolish player fails to respect opponents, and the inexperienced player tends to respect some opponents too much. The best pre-match preparation is a matter of working to obtain the proper balance. This enables you to give your opponent the credit if you lose, and to be a gracious winner if you win.

The following table summarizes how performance is affected by pre-match conceptions:

	TOO LITTLE RESPECT (I'M GOOD, YOU'RE NOT)	TOO MUCH RESPECT (I'M NOT GOOD, YOU ARE)	BALANCE OF RESPECT (I'M GOOD, YOU'RE GOOD)
MY BAD SHOT	↓	—	—
MY GOOD SHOT	—	ZONING ↑	—
MY OPPONENT'S BAD SHOT	—	↑ OR ↓	— ↑
MY OPPONENT'S GOOD SHOT	↓	—	— ↑
MY STATE OF MIND	↓ = POOR PLAY	UP AND DOWN = UNRELIABLE PLAY	BEST & MOST RELIABLE PERFORMANCE

Figure 9-2. Pre-match state of mind.

Figure 9-3 shows the flow and direction that a match will most likely take as a result of the three different attitudes toward an opponent that can be taken before entering a match.

The ideal approach to win a two-set match would be similar to the approach of a runner preparing for a two-mile race. The runner should start quickly, but settle soon into a comfortable stride. The runner should keep a steady, brisk pace for the greater part of the race, keeping enough left over for a finishing kick.

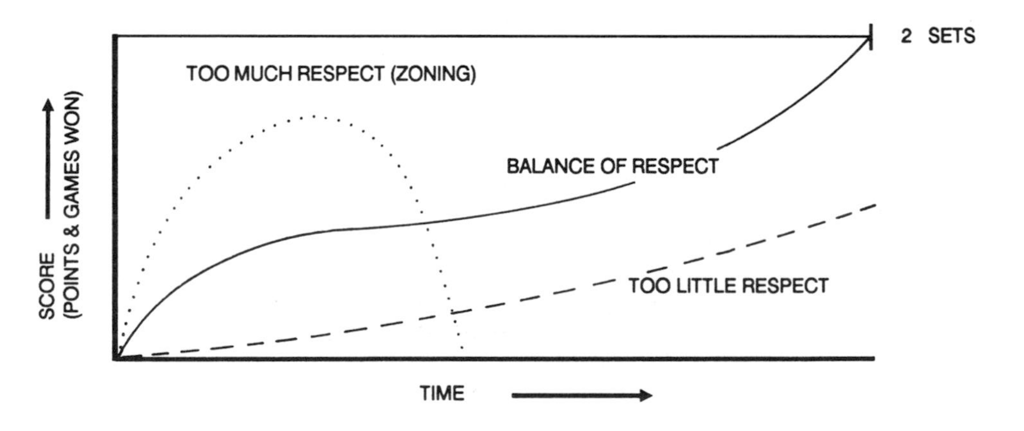

Figure 9-3. The influence of attitude toward the opponent.

Respecting an opponent too much is similar to the runner who goes out too fast and sprints to an early lead, but collapses quickly when things get close. Tennis players assuming this role often play all their best shots early in the match. A good opponent is not threatened by great shots early in the match, and recognizes that a player who starts this way often does not have anything left when the points get critical.

Having a lack of respect for an opponent is similar to the runner who starts the two-mile race in a jog and falsely believes he or she can catch up later. This lack of readiness usually leads to a too-little, too-late scenario.

During match play, competitors must trust their motor skills.

"In action, be primitive;
in foresight, a strategist."

— René Char

10

Keeping it Simple

Everyone says you are supposed to use your head in tennis, but what does that really mean? The confusion over what to think about on the court starts when the novice player finds his or her strokes, which had worked so well earlier on the practice court, suddenly delivering error after error. The response usually is to start analyzing the mechanics of the stroke. By this time, the opponent is well on the way to a victory.

Even experienced players make the critical mistake of "paralysis by analysis" during match play. Just as musicians cannot worry about technique in the middle of a recital, tennis players must understand that match play is not the time to worry about stroke mechanics. The fine motor skills of the athlete cannot work if the athlete is nervously sending messages to the muscles to do this or to do that.

The best results are achieved during match play if you "trust" your motor skills. Nothing really can be done about changing a stroke during competition. You must play the match with the tool box of skills that you brought to the match. The strokes and timing will feel better on some days than on others. The goal is to go with the best that you have on that day. Your thoughts should focus on strategy and ball placement first, and then tempo and other details, such as keeping the hands relaxed, so that the motor skills can work. Stroke mechanics should have been addressed during practice; nothing much can be done about them during a match.

I make it clear to my players that during practice they practice, trying to perfect the mechanics and timing of their games by hitting thousands of balls. On game day they should focus on winning, using every fair tool they have, physically, mentally, and emotionally. They must trust their skills; if their physical tools aren't good enough, they must rely on their mental and emotional assets. The physical skills can be improved at the next practice.

Shot Selection Made Easy

The term "paralysis by analysis" is often appropriate in regard to shot selection. Just as professional playbooks for basketball and football teams aren't practical for beginning and intermediate athletes, strategies used by tennis professionals cannot be used effectively by players at the high school and club level.

Novice and intermediate players should focus primarily on stroke technique and consistency. After consistency is achieved, they can concentrate on shot selection and simple strategies. Too often, beginners' strategies consist of hitting to the backhand and to the forehand on alternating shots.

With shot selection, only two choices can be made. Do you change the direction of the ball? Do you not change the direction of the ball?

Novices should realize that fewer errors are made when they do not change the direction of the ball, because they are hitting the ball at a right angle to the target with a flat racquet face — in other words, they are hitting the ball back from where it came. This also gives the opponent fewer opportunities to make them run.

Therefore, not changing the direction of the ball is an effective strategy for difficult shots such as the return of serve, first passing shots, first volleys and any ball that is difficult to reach.

Changing direction of the ball, of course, forces the opponent to run, but you should keep an old saying in mind: "If you give an angle, you'll get an angle." To hit to the open court means you might have to do a lot of running yourself.

Your best shot selection strategy, therefore, might be to not change the direction of the difficult shots, and only go to the open court when the ball sits up enough for a forcing shot to be effective.

With practice, you will discover which shot selection patterns work best for you, and which work best when playing particular opponents. Remember, you only have two choices to make: to change the direction of the ball, or not to change the direction of the ball?

As you gain experience, you will discover a shot selection strategy that is best for you. You will be particularly adept at some shots, and weak in others. It is important to recognize these as soon as possible to help you understand and formulate your playing style.

You will not be good at every shot, so realize your strengths and learn how to use them in competition. Matches usually are won by those players who use their strengths and favorite shots during the contest.

Using Checkpoints

It can be confusing for coaches and players, even advanced players, to know exactly what to look for as a match develops. Players often rely chiefly on instincts, or they may tend to concentrate only on stroke production. But how much should players rely on their natural instincts, and how much should they rely on a logical plan of action?

I have a simple formula that addresses this concern, one that involves concentrating on *patterns, flow, and hands.*

Before a match, ask yourself these questions:

- What *patterns* am I trying to use?
- Am I managing the match *flow* and momentum?
- Can I stay relaxed so that the fine motor skills of my *hands* will work under pressure?
- Performance can be divided into three areas of concern: the physical, mental, and emotional. These provide important checkpoints. In the physical-technical area, game style matchups and court positioning are the checkpoints; in the mental area, running the correct play is the concern, and in the emotional area, it is maintaining a balance between being intense and relaxed, and handling the high and low points of a match without overreacting.

Physical checkpoints

The variables of planning strategy can be complex. Prematch preparation should focus on understanding the tools (skills) that are available to you and those available to your opponent. Your first responsibility is to use your basic tools and execute your game plan, because strategies against your opponent are useless unless your game is in proper working order.

Strategies often fail because a player's tools are insufficient or because a player abandoned those tools early in the match. You should lock in your style first, and then work to derail your opponent. This means delivering balls your opponent dislikes while getting shots that are your favorites. It is of great value during a match to expose an opponent's weakness, but this only works if you are on top of your game.

Changes in a player's body language, intensity, and stroke production are usually obvious. But more subtle changes may occur in a player's court positioning, and this is an extremely important physical aspect to watch for. If two players were to rally and hit ground strokes on an open parking lot instead of on a tennis court with all its restrictive dimensions, they probably would discover that their normal shots travel approximately the same distance every time, perhaps 65 or 70 feet. This is because the player's strokes have been developed within the normal court dimensions (a tennis court is 78 feet long).

You can gain many advantages if you play even one step closer to the net. First, your shots to your opponent are deeper, which forces the opponent's ball to be shorter. This enables you to be offensive minded, and forces your opponent to be defensive. You also gain better angles, because you do not have to cover as much of the court. The greatest benefit, though, is that it prevents your opponent from setting up and taking charge of the point.

You can force your opponent into a defensive position in one of two ways: hit the ball harder, or take the ball earlier. It is extremely difficult, if not impossible, to make yourself hit the ball harder than you are used to while still maintaining control. A much better approach is to take your shots a bit earlier and to maintain a confident stroke, which makes your opponent rush.

The main disadvantage of taking balls early is that you have less reaction time. You therefore should hit the ball without changing the direction of its flight to reduce the margin for error.

Mental checkpoints

After the physical checkpoints are in order, the next checkpoint is a mental or strategic procedure: Which play should be run?

The answer to this question is less obvious in tennis than in other sports. Often, at the critical stages of a match, tennis players focus only on their technical skills. This is wrong. Game time is not the time to worry whether or not your strokes are there; you've got to use whatever was in your tool box at the start of the match. Top basketball players do not worry about how their jump shot looks with a minute left in the game, nor does a quarterback think about his throwing release.

In tennis, though, players tend to overanalyze and pick out microscopic technical flaws in their games when they should be thinking only of which play they should run. Again, "paralysis by analysis" can be a fatal disease for an athlete in the heat of battle. It is more important to use momentum principles (outlined in the following chapter) to take charge of the match.

Emotional checkpoints

If you have chosen the correct technical way to play, have worked to control court positioning, and know which play to run, you have covered the checkpoints for playing a solid match. The final, key ingredient that enables all these things to work is making sure you are in the right "emotional zone." In other words, do you have the correct balance of pressure, as discussed in the previous chapter.

During the first two or three games of a match, you will make winning shots and errors, as will your opponent. You can gauge your emotional state by noticing your reaction to these events.

If you are in a good frame of mind to compete, you will react positively to your good shots, and shrug off your poor shots. Your opponent's good shots will not bother you, and you will get a small lift from your opponent's bad shots.

If you are in a poor frame of mind for competition, you will become upset with your poor shots and your opponent's winners, while taking no satisfaction in the good things that happen. After this cycle starts, it is difficult to reverse. This is a major checkpoint for emotional balance on the court.

Set goals and objectives for your performance, never expectations. Always give yourself something to gain in competitive situations. Remember, good things that happen should be viewed positively. Bad things that happen should be viewed as no worse than neutral occurrences. Viewing good things as neutrals and bad things as negatives because of poor expectations or perceptions usually leads to defeat.

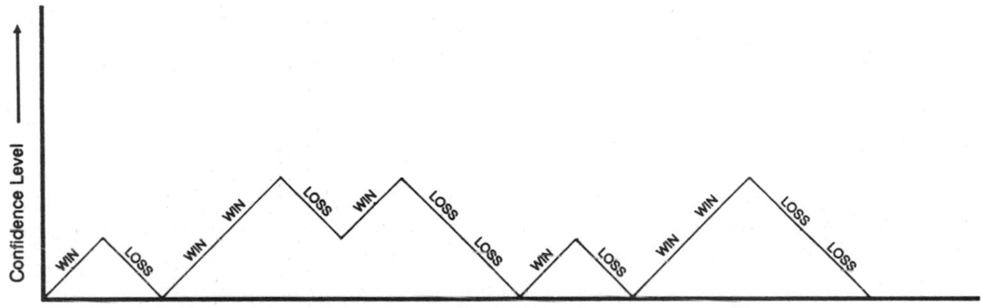

Figure 10-1. Poor response to wins and losses.

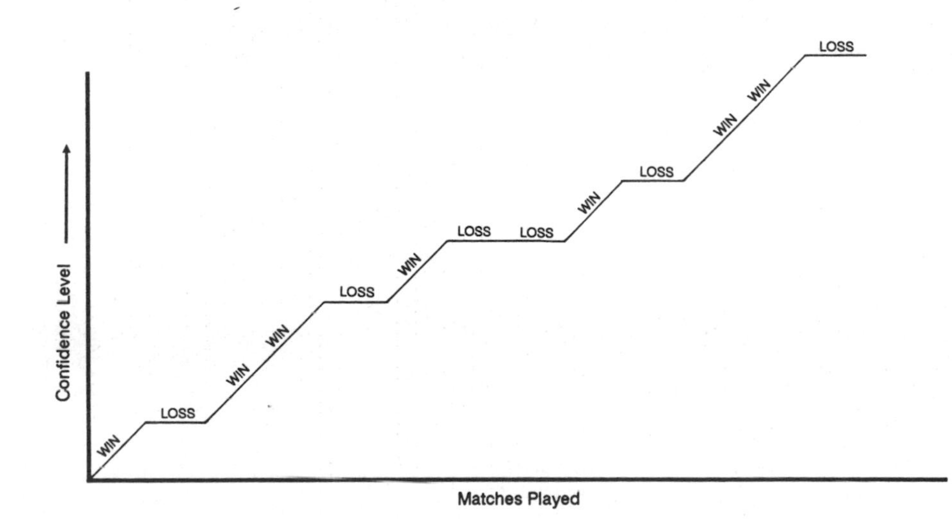

Figure 10-2. Best response to wins and losses.

Pancho Gonzalez had the intensity and stamina to endure momentum swings.

"If the enemy leaves a door open,
you must rush in."
— Sun Tzu

11

Controlling Momentum

In the summer of 1978, I sat with a coaching friend watching a major league baseball game. The game, a dramatic 12-inning battle, had many changes of fortune, as each team wasted opportunities. Finally, in the bottom of the 12th, a simple base hit drove in the deciding run.

As the up-and-down swings continued, the sports announcers constantly spoke of momentum. Good fortune would be with a team, then it would jump to the other team. My friend looked at me and said, "If as a coach you could ever learn a system to keep the momentum when you have it, and shut it down when your opponent has it, you would have the key to sports." That day I started my 15-year quest to try to learn how to control this seemingly magical power.

Stefan Edberg's U.S. Open victory in 1992 was remarkable because of the many momentum swings he had to endure. Match after match, he fought back from impossible odds as he won many five-set matches on his way to a second straight Open championship. His semi-final victory over Michael Chang was the most dramatic, as he fought from a 4-1 deficit in the fifth set to win. Tennis fans around the world saw the power of momentum at work.As tennis players become adept at their stroking skills and begin to think about strategy, they recognize that the decisions they make on the court are as important as their ability to execute a stroke.

At the beginning levels of strategy, game plans tend to focus on shot selection and patterns to use against opponents, such as where to serve, where to hit ground strokes and which of the opponent's strokes are vulnerable to attack.

After these strategies are learned, the next step is to manage the flow of the match by applying momentum control guidelines. Professionals are experts at managing momentum, but at every level players can make big strides in their match play if they learn to harness this power.

Tennis, more than any other sport, is a game of momentum. The absence of a clock to do the dirty work of finishing off an opponent, and the scoring system, makes the flow of the match of utmost importance.

In other sports, momentum can sometimes be controlled. Basketball coaches are perhaps the most adept at shutting down "Mo." They have their players pressure the opponents at times and back off at other times, hoping to frustrate their opponents into making mistakes. All too often in tennis, strategy is planned around an opponent's weakness, and match tempo is dictated by how a player is feeling. This would be absurd in any other sport, yet in tennis even the best players go into matches with the assumption that the outcome rests on their technical skills alone.

The most powerful skill that a singles or doubles player can learn and apply during competition is the ability to manage momentum. Sometimes a drastic change of events can influence momentum, such as a rain delay or an inj ury. These unplanned events can change momentum quickly and cannot be controlled. The athlete should understand that they do occur, and should be flexible enough to deal with the situation at hand.

Many aspects of momentum can be controlled, however. These are based on three variables in the match, as follows:

- The grouping of points (the conversion principle)
- The action taken when good shots and bad shots are made by you and your opponent (action-reaction principle)
- How the score affects the pressures (momentum principles based on the score)

Momentum and Match Flow Guidelines

The sequence in learning and controlling momentum and match flow should be as follows:

1. Conversion principles
2. Action-reaction principles
3. Momentum based on the score

The basic tools with which you have to work are *quick-pressure tactics* and *delayed-pressure tactics*. A quick, aggressive point forces your opponent to react immediately, whereas delayed pressure sets up the point more methodically. Quick-pressure points are also referred to as a "mo switch" and delayed-pressure points are referred to as break-down points.

Conversion principles

Bob Love, U.S.P.T.A. Master Professional, devised the conversion principles. To make a conversion means to win three points in a row; a double conversion is to win four in a row; a triple conversion is five points in a row, and so on.

Your first objective in controlling momentum is to make conversions and to prevent your opponent from doing so. Usually the best way to accomplish this is to recognize all two-point sequences won and lost and focus intently on the third point. Winning the conversion point is usually best achieved by using delayed-pressure tactics. Preventing the conversion point by your opponent is usually achieved by breaking the rhythm after the second point and to then use quick-pressure tactics.

Remember this motto: *Three in a row starts a flow.*

Note: Flow charting is an excellent tool to recognize conversions during a match. (See the following chapter.)

Action-reaction principles

Four actions can cause a reaction that is positive or negative when a point is played:

A great shot by your opponent. You should use quick pressure tactics to win the point back immediately, negating your opponent's momentum potential. *(Motto: If they give you a whack, hurt them right back.)*

A bad error by your opponent. Apply quick pressure to immediately increase the tempo of the points and to take the upper hand when your opponent is unsettled. *(Motto: If they make a careless mistake, a quick point try to take.)*

A great shot by you. Return to your fundamentals while maintaining an aggressive posture. Usually, a delayed pressure point should be played, but without playing tentatively. Tempo between points can be increased, but points should never be rushed. Quick targets should not be given to your opponent. *(Motto: If your shot has hurt them and they've started to bleed, delayed pressure to fester the wound is all you need.)*

Note: If your opponent reacts aggressively with success, follow the same guidelines and then return to delayed pressure tactics.

A bad shot by you. Take your time to regroup and return to the style and fundamentals in which you have confidence. *(Motto: If you bad shot has you in a fret, keep your poise, stick with fundamentals, and don't start until you're set.)*

If a point has been played where no momentum from action-reaction guidelines has taken place, use flow guidelines based on conversion principles or the following momentum guidelines based on score.

Momentum guidelines based on the score

It is a general principle of competition that an individual plays better and hits more aggressive shots when he or she is behind, and makes more mistakes by being tentative or rushing when ahead. This applies to games, sets and matches.

Most players tend to do only as much as they have to do to manage a situation, but good competitors play their best when their back is to the wall. Therefore, you should know how to use delayed-pressure tactics (breakdown points) and quick-pressure tactics (momentum-switch points).

To manage momentum swings that are caused by this changing pressure, observe the following rules:

- When you're ahead: Play smart and use more delayed pressure tactics, but continue to apply steady pressure.
- When you're behind: Play aggressive with more quick pressure tactics.
- When you're even: Go with your favorite style and have it locked in by the end of the match.

Observe the following mottos for momentum rules based on score:

- When you're in the lead, hurt your opponents early, then slowly make them bleed.
- When you're behind and you're trying to come back, keep your poise, have patience, but stay on the attack.
- When you're even it's crunch time, the rule is not so tough. Stay aggressive with your fundamentals, remembering that your regular stuff is always good enough.

Remember to use the rules of conversion principles, action-reaction principles, and momentum based on score in that sequence.

Momentum Mottos

In coaching young players, I have found it productive to give them the mottos already mentioned in this chapter for use when they are trying to manage the momentum of a match. The following is a summary of them:

A. Conversion Guidelines

- Three in a row starts a flow

B. Action-Reaction Guidelines

- If they give you a whack, try to hurt them right back.
- If they make a mistake, a quick point you should try to take.
- If your shot has hurt them and they start to bleed, delayed pressure to

fester the wound is all you need.

- If your bad shot has you in a fret, keep your poise, stay with your fundamentals, and don't start until you're set.

C. Score Flow Guidelines

- If you're in the lead, hurt your opponent early in the game, and then slowly make them bleed.
- If you're trying to come back, keep your poise, have patience, but stay on the attack.
- When it's crunch time, the rule's not so tough. Keep aggressive with your fundamentals, remembering that regular stuff is always enough.

Players have a lot of fun using these corny rhymes, and they are helpful in remembering what play to run under pressure.

Other factors can affect the momentum of a match as well. Some can be controlled, others cannot. It's important to be aware of them and know how to deal with them.

You should be aware of the following momentum changing and flow reversing factors:

- When opportunities to win games are not converted, especially large leads of two or three points.
- Rain delays
- Injury timeouts
- Bad calls by your opponent or by a linesman
- Emotional disruption by an opponent that may or may not cause a code violation.
- Code violations
- Equipment changes

To counter these obstacles, or take advantage of them, you must first be aware of the situation and then run the proper plays following the momentum guidelines.

Momentum is the most powerful force in sport. The more aware of it that you are, the more control you will have over the outcome of a match and the less prone you will be to a breakdown during a match.

Unemotional evaluation of performance fosters improvement.

"One cool judgement is worth a thousand hasty councils. The thing to do is to supply light and not heat."

— Woodrow Wilson

12

Evaluating Your Match

What happens after a match can be just as important as the procedure before the match. You put a great deal of time and preparation into preparing for and playing a match, so it is important to receive immediate and long-term feedback afterward. The way you handle this situation can hasten or delay your improvement.

Responding well to a loss is crucial for players. Some defeats are harder to take than others, and you must maintain a fine balance in your reaction. Discouragement and despair are not positive, nor is minimizing the loss and refusing to deal with it.

The greater your investment in a match, the more a loss hurts. If you take a loss too hard, however, you risk not making a full commitment for the next match. It is tempting to simply not try your hardest rather than run the risk of failing again.

One of the best things to do after a tough loss is go right back on the court and work out for 20 to 30 minutes. Some of my team's best practice sessions have taken place immediately following a crushing defeat. Two things are accomplished in these workouts: Anger and frustration are released, and the players leave the courts in a positive frame of mind, negating the negative impact of the loss.

The mental perspective of a loss cannot be discussed until the emotional and the physical aspects of it are addressed. It is best for the players to approach the strategic and technical parts of the match after their emotions have settled, even if it means waiting until the next day. Then, performances can be evaluated more effectively. A tough workout can serve as a physical release after a disappointing loss.

Victories present different challenges for the players. It is important to enjoy the victory, but to do so without gloating. After all, you probably have another match to play very soon. Victories should be enjoyed, but not to the extent that they interfere with your preparation for the next match. The emotional balance between confidence and humility is called "the zone," and you must find it before all matches to play your best.

The following guidelines can help you deal with wins and losses:

- Deal with the physical, the mental, and the emotional aspects of wins and losses.
- Losses are good opportunities to reinforce the positive in a player's game.
- The time following a loss can be a good time for a short and intense workout session.
- Enjoy your victories, but keep an emotional balance, so that you are prepared for your next match.
- Wait until the emotion of the match has settled for effective analysis.
- Try to keep winning and losing in the proper perspective.

Charting Systems for Match Play

Knowing what your objectives are before you chart a tennis match are critical to the effectiveness of a charting system. Charting a match, though, is one of the best ways to analyze your performance, because emotions often prevent you from seeing what is really happening.

A match chart can accomplish the following:

- Analyze which strokes were used.
- Identify the areas of the court that are producing missed shots.
- Analyze the amount of aggressive or forcing play in relation to your opponent.
- Study match flow.

The following two charting systems can be used to study these areas.

The Paul Scarpa charting system

Paul Scarpa, the tennis coach at Furman University, determined that in an average game, points were usually scored by hitting a winner, committing an unforced error, forcing an error from the opponent, or accepting an unforced error from the opponent.

This system shows winners, errors, forced errors, opponent's errors, the stroke used to win or lose the point, and the running score. The column that shows the forced errors is the most important, because the player who wins the match usually has a larger tally in this column. Figure 12-1 shows a sample Scarpa charting system tally sheet.

Player 1				vs	Player 2			
ERRORS	WINNERS	FORCED ERRORS	COACH'S COMMENTS	SCORE	ERRORS	WINNERS	FORCED ERRORS	COACH'S COMMENTS
F	S	S B		1–0	F	V_1		
B BR	FA	F		2–0	B V B			
F B V_1 S				2–1		BR		
	FB			3–1	B B	S		
F S*		B	*Double fault-game point!	3–2	F		B F	
	V			4–2				
	V S	V V		5–2		FP		
F B F FR*			* Poor game	5–3				
S	S V1	V		6–3	FR BR	O		
14	9	7		TOTALS	12	5	2	
				SET 2 ↓				

KEY

F = Forehand
B = Backhand
V = Volley
V_1 = First Volley
O = Overhead

S = Serve
BR = Backhand Return
FP = Forehand Pass
FR = Forehand Return
FA = Forehand Approach

Figure 12-1. The Paul Scarpa charting system tally sheet.

The Bob Love flow charting system

Bob Love's simplified flow charting system may be one of the easiest and most practical systems devised. Its main emphasis is the measurement of the flow and momentum of the match. In addition, it shows points won and lost, the stroke used to win or lose the point, conversions, and the running score.

Figure 12-2 shows a sample Bob Love charting system tally sheet.

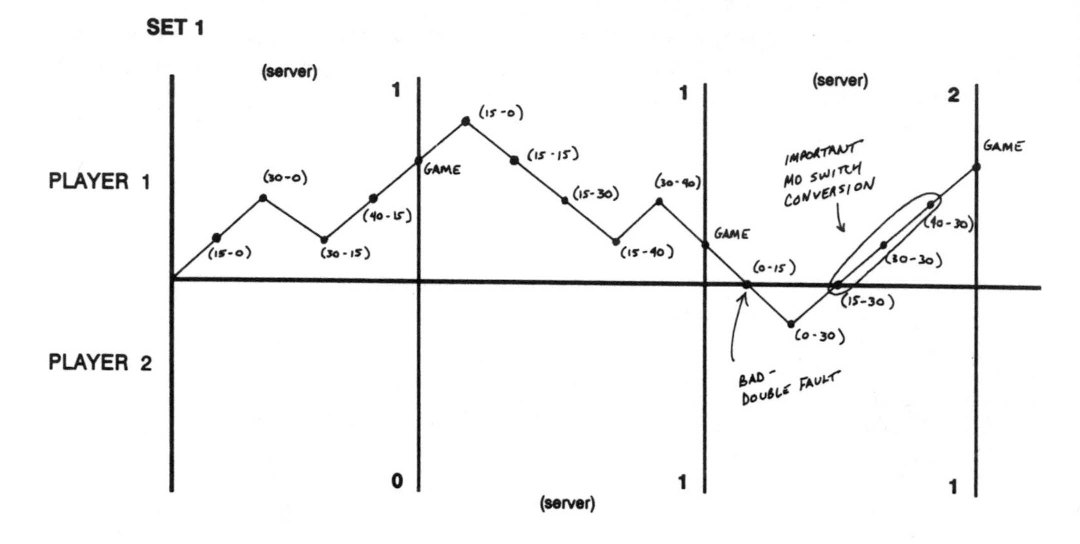

Figure 12-2. The Bob Love flow charting system tally sheet.

*"Nothing in the world can take the place of persistence.
Talent will not; nothing is more common than unsuccessful men with talent.
Genius will not; unrewarded genius is almost a proverb.
Education will not; the world is full of educated failures.
Persistence and determination alone are omnipotent."*

— Calvin Coolidge

Locking Your Back Door

I call it Tiger Pride, my athletes call it Morning Madness. For two weeks before the season starts, we gather at 6 a.m. to run. To make the team, each member must run a mile within 5 minutes, 15 seconds. One year at the end of the trials, only one boy had not qualified. Cris, who was 5 foot, 8 inches and a diabetic, had tried valiantly eight times, but his personal best was eight seconds too slow.

I was bombarded with pleas by Cris' teammates to make an exception. If any kid ever deserved it, he did. But on the tennis court and in the real world, Cris would not be competing only against small diabetics. I reaffirmed to him that a 5:15 mile was the only way to make the team. He agreed without reservation. I think we both knew this would be the last attempt.

With two upperclassmen, Greg and Mike, and a ball of kite string, we made one more try. I tied the string around the waist of each of the two "pacers," leaving 15 feet of slack. Cris would hang on to the end of each string as Greg and Mike alternately set the pace. I told Cris, "when you're at the end of your rope, tie a knot and hang on." If the string broke, Cris lost. Dropping it meant he had quit.

The pacers did their job. Greg ran the first two laps in 2 minutes, 30 seconds. Mike then took over. Lap 3 was the back-breaker. The string became taut down the backstretch as Cris struggled to keep up.

"No!" I yelled, "one more tough minute!" *There's a chance*, I thought to myself.

As Cris rounded the final backstretch, I knew he would make it. He fell across the finish line in 5:11, four seconds under the cutoff.

I let out a shout of joy, then laughed outrageously as I ran with Cris on his victory lap. This stumbling block to making the team had been overcome by a strong-minded kid, his coach, supportive friends and 30 feet of string.

Removing the Limitations

The fine line between achievement and failure in sports almost always lies in the limitations that athletes put on themselves. These are imposed by past experiences or by the athlete's environment.

In our sophisticated world of biomechanical analysis and highly-developed technical skills, motivation remains the most important aspect in achieving excellence.

Motivational techniques can run the gamut from simple to sophisticated, from a string tied around the waist of two teammates to a machine costing thousands of dollars. They can come in the form of a pat on the back or a kick in the butt.

The coach's job is to discover which tool works best for each athlete, but the objective of any motivational technique is the same: *To bring the athlete to the point of commitment.*

After athletes make a complete commitment to their sport, the coach's job becomes a much easier task of guiding them along the path of success. Without this commitment from the athlete, the coach's job is frustrating and tedious. Dr. Bill Moore, a sports psychologist, states, "Commitment means 'locking your back door,' and full success cannot be realized in any endeavor without it."

That sounds easy enough, but commitments are difficult to make because they involve risk. A 100 percent effort can bring success and elation, it also can result in defeat and great pain. Human nature tends to lead us to partial commitments, where the risk of the pain is lessened, but unfortunately the thrill of winning might be lessened as well.

Solving this age-old problem is the key to motivation. I tell my athletes that losing hurts whether they make a full commitment or not. The difference is that the pain of a loss from a full commitment is much like the pain of training the body. The lungs burn and the muscles ache, but growth comes from it. The pain of losing in a partial effort is much like a sickness or disease; even after recovery, the body is still weak from the pain.

The Risk of Commitment

Many competitive tennis players play the sport for years without making a commitment to the game or to themselves. The most frustrating and difficult thing for a coach is to try to induce those athletes to make a total commitment.

How do you get them to try harder? How do you convince them to use their talent to the fullest?

Teaching the value of commitment is often the greatest gift a coach can give to athletes. The ability to make a commitment will be with them throughout their lives, whether it's on a job, in a marriage, or in adherence to a religion. In America today we can satisfy 70 to 80 percent of our needs and achieve 70 to 80 percent of our potential without a commitment. Mediocrity can bring a lot of awards in a prosperous society, without taking many risks, but but the last 20 to 30 percent that brings total success cannot be achieved without a total commitment.

Players often try to delay making a commitment by relying more and more on talent. The greater the natural ability, the longer the procrastinatation. Less talented athletes are more likely to make a total commitment sooner in their careers out of necessity.

I try to teach my players the 3 D's of every challenge. First, they must have the **d**ream. At some point they will encounter **d**isappointment. Then they must choose between **d**iscovery and **d**iscouragement.

Use Your Ability, Desire and Opportunities

Three ingredients are necessary for success in tennis and in most other sports: *ability, desire,* and *opportunity*. Many unsuccessful athletes have two of these ingredients, but all three are essential to reach peak performance. You cannot do it on your own, but neither can anyone else do it for you.

Ability is the God-given part of an athlete's makeup. If you are born with a four-cylinder engine, then you cannot run on six or eight cylinders. Your size, speed, strength, coordination, and instinct are accidents of birth, and each has a maximum capacity for development. These gifts may be great or small, but usually fall somewhere between. Their development is based on your desire and opportunity.

Desire is your responsibility, for it is your choice whether to develop or to neglect the ability that you possess. In the early stages of training, parents, teachers, coaches, or friends can coax you into improving your skills, but ultimately you determine your development. Desire is the basis of motivation. How to instill desire is a mystery that is rarely solved, but in the end it is always up to the individual athlete.

Opportunity is relative, but necessary. Players must know how good they have to be before they can be properly motivated. Tennis is so bound by the pecking order and ranking philosophy that, without opportunity and exposure, growth can easily stagnate.

Exposure keeps players hungry by letting them know how good they have to be, what they have to work on, who they must be able to beat and what other players are doing to improve. It may be detrimental that rankings carry so much influence on the pecking order of tennis players. In other sports, athletes are usually rated on their skills rather than on how much exposure they have received. In tennis, players need exposure, and growth comes from the opportunities that exposure presents.

Opportunities are plentiful for tennis players in the U.S. Many of our young athletes have too many opportunities available to them with little or no effort on their part. Parents and coaches, aware that opportunities are an important element in any athlete's growth, often supply them before athletes have paid their dues. In America, we are so enthusiastic about providing opportunities that we often prevent people from making their own way, thus crippling their best talent.

Coaches and athletes should recognize the critical ingredients of reaching potential. Ability, desire, and opportunity are essential for an athlete's growth, but the responsibility for each of them comes from different sources. Ability is God's job, desire is the athlete's job, and opportunity is the parent's, teacher's, or coach's job. One quote I always have loved reads as follows: "What we are is God's gift to us. What we become is our gift to God."

The P.E.P.P. Motivational Program

Every athlete should have an intelligent, specific and thorough training program and stick with it. The P.E.P.P. program can provide direction to athletes, and can be used as a plan for other challenges that require discipline and direction. P.E.P.P. covers training from the planning phase through the actual execution and success.

P (Preparation): The Athlete's First Objective

Bob Knight, coach of three NCAA basketball championship teams at Indiana University, said it best: "More important than the will to win is the will to *prepare* to win."

Without physical and mental preparation, an athlete has little or no hope for success. Preparation is the base that has to be laid before an athlete steps onto the court or playing field. An athlete's preparation must be detailed and thorough. It must include complete programs of training for the body, mind, and spirit so that at its conclusion the athlete is mentally, physically, and emotionally ready for the job at hand. A good training program provides tremendous confidence; lack of one leaves success almost totally to fate.

Step one: Have a burning desire

Nearly every athlete would claim to want to be successful. But simple desire is different than burning desire. This intangible difference separates good from great, the mundane from the memorable. Burning desire cannot be given to an athlete, it must come from within. The athlete who has a burning desire will endure the training and hardships met along the way.

Step two: Set specific goals

Nearly all athletes and coaches set goals. Some goals are unrealistic and never realized, while others are almost always reached. Some direct athletes to maximize their talent, while others offer no significant challenges. What is the key to setting goals?

Achieving potential depends on setting the *correct* goals — objectives that motivate an athlete to give 100 percent effort while achieving some success along the way. Goals that are set properly should be reached only about 50 or 60 percent of the time. Athletes should compare an idealistic outlook with a totally realistic outlook and find a point midway between the two in determining goals.

Goals should constantly be reset and redirected. It is best to set three goals for an objective: a long-term goal that is the ultimate objective (the thought of which keeps the flame of desire bright), an intermediate goal that is a year or so away (to remain on course toward the main goal), and short-term goals that constantly provide smaller successes and failures (to keep enthusiasm and learning stimulated for the ultimate objective).

A high correlation exists between athletic success, intellectual success, and social success. Goals therefore should be set in other areas besides sports, including academics, social areas, family areas, career planning, finance and spiritual areas. Success in each of these areas supports and aids the development of the others.

Step three: Be constructive and positive

Working hard is necessary to achieve goals, but it is not a guarantee of success. Hard work increases the chance of success, and gives you peace of mind in knowing that you have done everything in your power to prepare yourself for the challenge. Thinking that hard work should guarantee success, however, distorts motives for competing and can cause frustration if the results are disappointing.

Many people work hard for the wrong reason: they are result-oriented and think only of the reward. I call this "outside-in" work. This work is not productive because it is not inspired or creative. It results in frustration, and the successes that are sometimes achieved may not be fulfilling. However, working for the love of it, or pursuing a calling as an expression of one's self ("inside-out" work), inspires countless successes. As the saying goes, "great athletes compete to express, not impress."

Athletes should work hard and sacrifice, but they should do so for the right reasons. Love of one's work and enjoyment of the accomplishments that might result from it are the keys to longevity in a career. Working from the inside-out rather than outside- in keeps the motivational fires burning for a long time.

Step four: Take care of details

Athletes and coaches often throw away months or years of hard work by neglecting to take care of details. An athlete may have a burning desire, may set the most specific and appropriate goals, and may work in a dedicated fashion to prepare for a match, but all can be wasted by neglecting seemingly insignificant details. An athlete should pay attention to simple items such as eating properly, getting adequate sleep, being properly equipped and warming up correctly.

Step five: Acknowledge nervousness

One of the best things the athlete can do prior to performance is face up to fear. Just as failure generally precedes success, fear can be viewed as a prelude to the positive emotion of courage, because courage is a reaction to fear. Athletes should acknowledge fear so that it can be dealt with and used productively. To disregard fear allows it to grow, leading to the negative emotions of doubt, worry, anxiety, and frustration, which hinder performance.

Fear of competition does not always exist. Children usually are not susceptible to it until they reach the age of 10 or 12. This is about the age when pressure becomes noticeable and children start reasoning logically about the rewards or consequences of their behavior. Sometimes outside pressures are more than a youngster is capable of handling. For this reason, the pressures involved in competitive sports should increase gradually with the young athlete's ability to understand them.

Another no-fear situation occurs when an athlete attempts to ignore the pressure of the event and pretends not to care about the outcome. This is one reason why not all athletes show commitment to their sport. They feel that if they don't risk, they can't lose. Unfortunately, athletes who do not risk do not gain, either. Many athletes apparently would rather have success come their way by good fortune than by taking an active role in making it happen.

E (Enthusiasm): The Spirit Behind Performance

The word enthusiasm comes from the Greek *en theos*, which means "the spirit of God within." The meaning of the word describes its importance to anyone working in a creative field. Inside-out, or true, enthusiasm is inspired, whereas outside-in, or false, enthusiasm is forced. The latter is seldom helpful. The former should always benefit performance.

Athletics is perhaps the purest and most expressive of all art forms. Through sports, the inner self can be totally released in a creative manner. Athletes often inhibit this inner creativity and hold back their opportunity to express the inner self through performance.

Perhaps the greatest benefit of enthusiasm is that it projects confidence, and true confidence always overcomes fear. Enthusiasm, in fact, often makes the opposition fearful. Most athletes do not counter with enthusiasm when confronting an enthusiastic opponent. Instead, they become more passive. Many matches or games are lost for this reason.

Enthusiasm is increasingly difficult to generate as a task becomes routine. Even the most exciting experience has a tendency to become boring after awhile. The true test for an athlete, or anyone for that matter, is to maintain enthusiasm long after the novelty has worn off. Great players and coaches usually are able to perform their jobs each year with the same eagerness and enthusiasm, and consequently they are able to grow and attain higher levels of development. Enthusiasm coupled with the experience of a veteran makes a great combination.

P (Poise): The Mark of an Experienced Athlete

Poise is the ability to execute one's skills regardless of the pressure of the situation. It is an important skill to have, and great athletes exhibit it time and time again. In fact, poise is learned by experiencing pressure situations and responding to them in a positive fashion.

It is difficult to teach poise, but a few guidelines can help the athlete develop it in the heat of the battle:

- Growth occurs best amid adversity and tough competition, so athletes should look forward to pressure-filled situations; they can only better prepare the athlete to be less fearful in the future.
- Creativity occurs best when a person is in a relaxed state. Creative talents are never forced to the surface. Writers, artists, and musicians often retreat to a hideaway so that their creative talents can flow and surface. With poise, athletes can bring their creativity to the surface even under adverse situations.
- The key to continuous growth in athletics is to treat success and failure in the same manner. This helps an athlete develop poise and confidence. The normal tendency after a success is to let the emotions run sky high. Likewise, the tendency after a setback is for the emotions to bottom out in grief and anxiety. Competitors should learn never to get too high over a win or too low over a loss. This is not to say that one should not be happy over a win or disappointed over a loss, but a balance between the two is critical for development. If excuses are not made, if losses are accepted as the athlete's own responsibility, and if positive qualities are recognized, maximum growth occurs.

Remember: *Winning is a chance for confidence; losing is a chance for growth.*

An athlete must learn to maintain a balance between enthusiasm and poise. This balance can be obtained by practicing concentration. The optimal situation would be for the rookie to have the poise of a veteran and the veteran to have the enthusiasm of a rookie.

P (Perseverance): The Power of Commitment

Some people achieve greatness because of perseverance alone. The ability to face all adversity and to keep trying is the final quality all great athletes must have.

Many people see only the glory that goes with being a star athlete. It is difficult to see the hardship one must experience to achieve that greatness. The hardships, however, are what mold the great athletes. The confidence that is obtained from those struggles propels athletes to greater heights. They fear little because they have conquered much.

Many people give up after two or three unsuccessful attempts. They don't realize that the wisdom and experience gained from pursuing a goal are more important than short-term gratification, and lead to greater opportunities in the future. One can only imagine Thomas Edison's perseverance as he failed again and again in his attempt to make an electric light bulb. Each time a player has a setback on the tennis court, it is like Edison's light bulb flickering and going out again. The player with perseverance finds a way to keep the bulb lit. Remember, it was Edison who said, "Genius is one percent inspiration and 99 percent perspiration."

Another of my favorite quotes regarding perseverance is from Winston Churchill, who said, "To each man there comes a time when an opportunity presents itself that is specifically designed for those talents and gifts of the man. What a tragedy when this time comes and finds the man unprepared to take advantage of it."

In developing perseverance, a few reminders are helpful:

- Breakdowns always occur before breakthroughs.
- Setbacks are the clay from which all great people are molded.
- Each person has his or her own unique timetable for success. Never compare your successes with another person's, for this leads only to frustration. Keep working at your own rate.
- Another person's accomplishments never make you look bad. Jealousy is a negative emotion and nothing positive can be gained by it. Be happy for others' successes.
- Be disappointed, but never discouraged.
- Know the difference between quitting and changing direction. Quitting is running away from a threatening situation and avoiding responsibility. Changing direction is moving to a beneficial new path. Change direction 100 times in your lifetime if you must, but never quit.

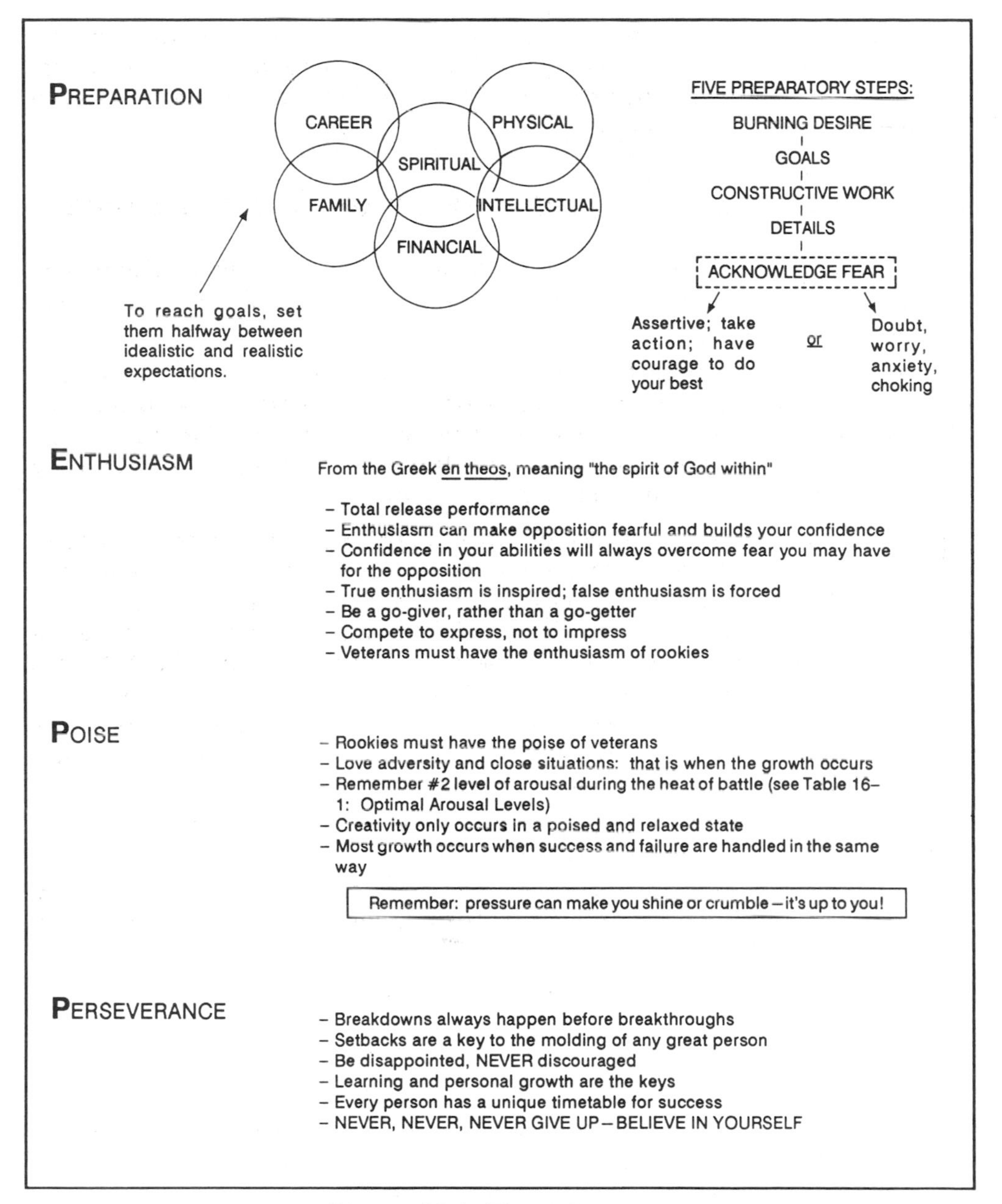

Figure 13-1. The P.E.P.P. system.

Getting Up for the Game

As I was growing up and competing in tennis and other sports, I strongly believed that the harder I tried, the more successful I would be. If I lost I felt guilty, figuring I must not have tried hard enough. Sadly, many athletes feel the same way and constantly berate themselves for being lazy when things are going poorly, often until their self-image and confidence are torn down.

Can someone try too hard? As a youngster, I used to play my best friend, Lester, in match after match. I got very fired up for each one, but it didn't matter. We met at least 15 times, and I lost by close straight-set scores each time. The thing that always got to me was that he appeared not to be trying. He moved smoothly from corner to corner, threading passing shots just past me, always getting one more ball back until I cracked. I always responded by saying to myself, "I'll just work harder." My level of arousal when I competed was about the same as that of a pro football linebacker, and Les always acted as nonchalant as someone sunbathing on the beach. I could not understand or accept the unfairness of this situation.

It was not until I was 24 years old and taking a course in graduate school that I learned about optimal levels of arousal for different sports. Try too hard? I had not thought that was possible. I believed an athlete should always try 110 percent. My emotional level was so high when I competed that I would physically tie up and choke. This high level of arousal also hampered my mental processes, and I was unable to think clearly, making myself subject to the roller-coaster ride of my emotions.

The list in table 16-1 was shown to me in a graduate school class, and I have kept it to help athletes who do not focus their concentration properly in the heat of the battle. It is from an article by Joseph B. O'Xendine, called "Emotional Arousal and Motor Performance."

How tight? How loose?

Two personalities prevail in competitive sports: the diligent hard worker, and the person who is loose-as-a-goose. The former is obsessive and driven, and practices skills again and again and again. The latter is a cocky competitor who thinks he or she can do it all.

The athlete with the driven temperament has obvious advantages, and most coaches love to work with this athlete. The problem is that on game day this athlete usually tries too hard and often chokes. The cocky athlete appears to have everything under control on game day, but often fails to get the job done because of the lack of diligent training.

Bill Moore, a sports psychologist, helped our team by explaining that levels of arousal for practice day and match day should not be the same. It would be best if a player's personality were a combination of the two personalities — someone who is driven during practice to do everything necessary to improve skills but who on game day is able to approach the competition with an inwardly confident and outwardly cocky attitude. But athletes tend to be one way or the other, and find it difficult to change arousal levels from practice day to game day. The key for the driven athlete is to try hard in the right way on game day, which enables the fine motor skills to work. For the loose and cocky athlete, discipline and structure during practice promotes preparation that can make the difference during competition.

LEVEL OF AROUSAL	SPORTS SKILLS
5 (EXTREMELY EXCITED)	Football (blocking and tackling) Performance on the Rogers' PFI Test Running (220 yards to 440 yards) Sit up, push up, or bent arm hang test Weight lifting
4	Running long jump Running very short and long races Shot put Swimming races Wrestling and judo
3	Basketball skills Boxing High jumping Most gymnastic skills Soccer skills
2	Baseball (pitching and batting) Fancy dives Fencing Football (quarterback) Tennis
1 (SLIGHT)	Archery and bowling Basketball (free throws) Field goal kicking Golf (putting and short irons) Skating (figure eights)
0 (NORMAL STATE: NO EMOTION)	

Figure 13-2. Optimal arousal levels for some typical sports skills.

There are exceptions in every sport to the theory of the optimal level of arousal. And even an athlete who knows what level of emotional arousal produces the best performance might not be able to compete comfortably at that level. Each athlete must find his or her own optimal level of arousal and work to find that zone of emotional balance for competition.

The higher your reach, the greater your achievements.

"One ship sails East, one ship sails West,
no matter what the wind doth blow,
it's the set of the sail, not the force of the gail,
that determines where your ship will go."

— Ella Wheeler Wilcox

14

Getting What You Expect

In 1978, my third year of coaching, I learned that the coach's expectations can easily become the player's expectations if the coach does not let the players know the difference.

We should never have won the state collegiate tournament that year. Our No. 1 player, Mike Gandolfo, had a shoulder injury and was unable to compete. Our top freshman was unable to play because of a disciplinary action. We were left with a much weaker team, and we had to face very strong opposition from the best teams in South Carolina.

The team that we would field for the tournament consisted of three freshmen and two sophomores, only one of whom had much playing experience. As I evaluated the situation, I realized there was no way in the world I could expect this team to finish among the top three teams; to think they could win the tournament was out of the question.

I had two options: I could expect nothing out of my team and be pleasantly surprised if it did well, or I could flat-out lie to my players and tell them we had a great chance to win the tournament.

The tournament would be held on the clay courts of The Citadel in Charleston. I rationalized to the team that the two players sitting out were hard court players, and we now had our best clay court team entering the tournament. I told them that champions are made from adversity, and that because we had this adversity we would be in a prime position to win the championship.

I said, though, that the job would be tough. I set a specific goal for the first day of winning at least eight matches out of the nine flights. Regardless of how our team did, though, I told my players that one other team would play great the first day and win all nine flights. Our goal for the second day would be to have another solid day. Another team would also play great the second day; we would be in the money rounds, and on the third day the best-conditioned team would win. Because we had trained hard, it would pay off on this day.

As I talked with the guys, I thought to myself, "This is the biggest lie I have ever told in my life. There is no way in the world that these guys can win." Still, I thought this was the best of my two options.

My players believed me, and this taught me how important my expectations for them were. It also taught me that young people trust a person who is in a position of authority, especially if they respect that person. I learned that my job as a coach and a role model was a very important one.

To my disbelief, a few of the players who never should have won matches came through in the clutch, and we ended up winning eight matches the first day. South Carolina had a day equal to ours, and Furman won all nine of its matches and took an early lead in the tournament. That night, I told my players that we had accomplished our goal for the day. I told them that the second day would be a very tough day, and our goal for the second day was to have another solid performance. Once again, I wondered how I could tell my players we could accomplish such unrealistic things.

On the second day, the Furman team had a poor day, the South Carolina team won eight matches, and our team won seven matches. Again, I was surprised to have so many victories. That night in the meeting, I congratulated the players on reaching their goal for the day and explained to them that this was the way it was supposed to be. We were now in a position to win on the last day, and that had been our goal all along. I told them that we had worked to be in better condition than anybody else, and that the long matches on the clay had worn out many of the opponents. I also told my players that none of the matches would be easy, and that they would have to be at their best to win.

I still felt as if I was lying, and I didn't really give my team much chance of winning on the last day. My expectations were low, but somehow I put on a positive front. All of the matches were tough. In fact, five of them were three-setters, and three of those ended up 7-5 in the third. But the players came through in the clutch every time, and when they walked off, instead of happy jubilation, they took the wins with a matter-of-fact attitude — as if they were supposed to win.

As we won the deciding point to win the championship, I caught myself before I could let out a yell. I immediately walked about 100 yards away, stood behind a tree, and let out a scream. I thought about how I had told a whopper to my players and how I had so much less confidence in them than they had in themselves. We were certainly not the best team in the state tournament that year, and their confidence had merely come from the expectations that I had expressed to them. The bottom line, though, was that my players thought they were the best team, and that is why they won. I walked back onto the courts and did everything I could to contain my happiness, because I realized that if I were to celebrate outwardly too much, I might kill the momentum that we could develop as a team from that point on.

The Pecking Order of Expectations

Bill Hodges, Larry Bird's college basketball coach, once related to me an old story that shows the importance of self-image. It goes as follows:

A man found an eagle's egg and put it in the nest of a backyard hen. The eaglest hatched with the brood of chicks and grew up with them.

All his life, the eagle did what the backyard chickens did, thinking he was a backyard chicken. He scratched the earth for worms and insects. He clucked and cackled. And he would thrash his wings and fly a few feet in the air.

Years passed and the eagle grew very old. One day he saw a magnificent bird far above him in the cloudless sky. It glided in graceful majesty among the powerful wind currents, with scarcely a beat of its strong golden wings.

The old eagle looked up in awe. "Who's that," he asked.

"That's the eagle, the king of the birds," said his neighbor. "He belongs to the sky. We belong to the earth — we're chickens."

So the eagle lived and died a chicken, for that's what he thought he was.

Tennis is a tough sport because of its ranking system. The pecking order is quickly established, and players discover what achievements they are comfortable with. The pecking order is so rigid that I firmly believe if a player is not favored to win, that player usually will not win. It is fun to play the underdog role because it poses the unthreatening situation of having something to gain and nothing to lose, but it has been my experience that players who have nothing to lose generally lose.

The scoring system in tennis dictates that a player has to win a minimum of 48 "battles" (points) to win one match. To close out the other player, a player must be better by two points every game. It does not matter if one player is much more spectacular on point 21 or on point 37, that player must out-perform the opponent on the final two points of the match to win. The ingenious scoring system of tennis makes it difficult to score upsets.

Many books have been written about positive thinking and attitudes, and they all have a similar message: People are as they perceive themselves. Academic endeavors provide good examples of the effects of expectations on performance.

For example, one student has been an A student for quite some time. He or she makes A's again and again, arousing little or no surprise or excitement from anyone. Success is expected and accepted, so reward is sometimes neglected. When that student gets a B, it is a tremendous disappointment to everyone, and the student's feeling of failure is great.

Another student has a C average, and is comfortable in that role. But if that student makes two or three B's all of a sudden, everyone sings his or her praises. Note the different reactions for the same job by two different people, all because of the expectations placed on them.

If the C student then changes his or her behavior and studies more diligently than ever before and makes straight A's, everyone is thrilled. But if that student makes straight C's again the next semester, everyone wonders what happened. People are comfortable with the expectations to which they are accustomed; if someone achieves beyond those expectations, he or she may retreat to the previous level.

Achievement brings higher expectations, which brings more challenges and responsibility. It is obvious, then, why many players remain mediocre.

Overcoming the Pecking Order

Being the favorite has definite advantages in a tennis match. No matter how well you are prepared mentally, physically, and emotionally, you might run up against a more talented opponent. What are your options in this case? Not play? Concede that you probably will lose, but play the match anyway for experience? Go for broke and hope that something magical happens?

You should remember that 50 percent of a match's outcome has to do with how your opponent plays. It is critical to try to maintain your best play while staying within your limitations. Your goal, then, is to get your opponent to play at a lower level.

Stick to a basic game plan and follow these guidelines:

- Use only your tool box of skills.
- Keep good court positioning.
- Run the right plays (use the momentum control system).
- Keep emotional balance and proper reactions to the ups and downs in the match.
- Play with total trust and enthusiam in your style.
- Have a method for setting match goals and stick to the plan.

"Hold yourself responsible for a higher standard than anyone else expects of you. Never excuse yourself."

— Henry Ward Beecher

15

Eliminating Excuses

One January evening, after wishing my mother a happy birthday, I told her that I was upset with my team for making excuses and failing to accept responsibility.

"Young people nowadays," I said, "have the brashness to take a stand on anything, but few have the guts to accept responsibility. Why can't people just say, 'I screwed up, I'm sorry'? Why are there always 40 reasons why it happened?"

My mother calmed me and said, "Human nature is the same as it's always been. The only difference now is that society has provided people with reasons. Let me put it this way: Mrs. Brown who lives next door is an old battle-ax. Nowadays we look at Mrs. Brown and say, 'Poor Mrs. Brown, isn't it sad that her husband is an alcoholic, her daughter ran off with a teenage boyfriend, and her son is taking drugs? Poor Mrs. Brown. She's upset. She's nervous. She's got troubles.' But, hey! The bottom line is that Mrs. Brown is an old battle-ax, whatever the reasons."

I thought of the old woman who lived next door to our house when I was a child. There were six kids in our family, and the old woman would yell at us and steal our ball whenever it went into her yard. I knew what my mother was talking about. Perhaps today we might have found an elaborate way of giving this old woman some excuse for her behavior. I remembered thinking, though, "Wouldn't that be the wrong thing to do?" After all, it seemed that the role of battle-ax was something she was good at and almost enjoyed. Why rob her of it by giving her excuses for her actions? I also thought, "Hey! If we had looked hard enough, we could have found reasons for a lot of old women on the block to be battle-axes."

This story made me understand that one of the toughest jobs in coaching today is to get young players to take responsibility for their actions. Tennis is a difficult game to play. It is even more difficult to play well, and it is one of the hardest games to learn to win. But the biggest frustration I have as a coach is not that the physical and mental parts of the game are so difficult to learn, but that it is so difficult for the players to take the responsibility for their own play. It usually seems that the better the player, the more sophisticated the excuse for coming up on the short side in a match. The temptation to make an excuse will always be with a player, because tennis is such a hard game to play. Another coach once told me, "Excuses are like people's rear ends — everyone has one."

Defense Mechanisms

Sigmund Freud stated that sometimes a failure situation is so painful for a person that a defense mechanism is needed to preserve self-esteem. Unfortunately, though, a defense mechanism can seriously hinder athletic growth because it keeps a person from working to improve skills. I tell my players that after they take the court, there is no reason for a loss other than, "My opponent played better than I did." Once you take the court, that's all there is to say. If something is bothering you that much, don't take the court. Make no excuses once you take the court. If you're willing to take responsibility for the loss, you'll be more likely to want to get right back on the practice court and try again.

A player should be humble in victory and give full credit to the opponent in defeat, no matter how tough that might be. If, however, the loss is just too unbearable, I tell my players they at least should be familiar with the list of tennis excuses if they refuse to accept the blame.

Bill Bos, a former collegiate coach and currently a tennis pro in Dallas, wrote the following list of excuses for tennis players. It was a big help to me as a college athlete by providing a humorous outlet for my frustrations, and helping me focus on what really was important — my game.

- Ate too much lunch.
- Did not eat enough.
- Drank too much water.
- Favorite racquet broke.
- Needed new balls.
- Balls too light.
- Balls too heavy.
- Balls too fuzzy.
- Net was too high.

- Net was too low.
- The racquet was slipping in my hand.
- Opponent was ranked.
- Tournament director didn't seed me.
- Opponent didn't play tennis, just hit the ball back.
- Opponent was so bad I couldn't play my game.
- I didn't realize opponent was left-handed until the next-to-the-last game.
- I just couldn't get into it today.
- These strings just don't give me the power I need.
- How can I be expected to play my best on these courts?
- This injury keeps me from playing well.

Excuses such as these are well-understood by players, because all of us have resorted to them during our careers. They can be a fun thing for current players. My team members are quick to pick up on another team member's attempt to make an excuse, even if it is a valid one, and to label it. In nearly all cases, it makes a positive situation out of a painful loss.

Once, when an impending loss was overbearing, my dying brother-in-law read "Rockne's Prayer" to me. Now, the words of the prayer are with me always as I go into competition. It reads:

Lord, in the struggle that goes on through life,

We ask for a field that is fair,

A chance that is equal,

With all this strife,

And the courage to strive and to dare.

And, if we should win,

Let it be by the code,

With our honor held high.

But if we should lose,

Let us stand by the road,

And cheer as the winners go by.

This philosophy epitomizes the best attitude that one could ever have for competition. The point is, don't make excuses, take responsibility.

Net skills are a crucial component of doubles play.

"If anything goes bad, then I did it.
If anything goes semi-bad, then we did it.
If it goes real good, then you did it."

— Paul "Bear" Bryant

16

Training Doubles Skills

With four players instead of two covering just a bit more court than in a singles match, the doubles match relies more heavily on court positioning than on shot-making. Shot-making seems to be of greater importance in singles play because there a player can be forced off balance and out of position more easily. In singles, the court position to shot-making ratio could be rated at about 65 percent to 35 percent; in doubles it is probably just the opposite: 35 percent to 65 percent.

The doubles game is also more repetitive than singles, and doubles players find themselves playing the same type of point again and again, whereas in singles it often seems that no two points are the same. Playing good doubles, then, is a matter of consistently executing fundamentals while being flexible enough to make a subtle change when needed.

The players' first task is to learn their specific jobs and responsibilities at each position they play on the court. Each player will play about one fourth of his or her points as the server's partner, and one fourth of his or her points as the receiver's partner. If each player knows his responsibility at each position, the doubles match can be played with much more confidence.

The specific jobs of server, server's partner, receiver, and receiver's partner should be worked on at every doubles practice until players understand them and can effectively carry them out. They are the fundamentals for playing doubles effectively and if learned well, establish a firm foundation that can be built upon.

The Fundamental Positions

The positions of server and receiver are the most crucial for a doubles team to be effective. It is critical that the server master the fundamentals of a good second serve and a solid first volley. It is equally important for the receiver to make a solid cross-court return.

These skills are so important that during the first two months of the season I have my team members play one-versus-one (invisible partner) doubles, or cross-court serve and volley matches where records are kept and results used to rank the players for later doubles pairings. Also, the players are only allowed one serve, which helps them learn an effective second serve under pressure.

The players get tired of playing the same cross-court game over and over, but after the second month they are skilled at second serves, first volleys, crosscourt returns, and quick volleys. Figure 16-1 shows the boundaries for these games. (My thanks to James Wadley, tennis coach at Oklahoma State University, for helping me to establish this approach to teaching doubles.)

The Server's Jobs

Job one: Make the first serve

This is the most basic job, because the receiver naturally thinks defensively on the first serve and offensively on the second serve. A big first serve about once a game works well to keep the receivers off balance and out of a groove, but a high percentage of first serves is critical to be successful.

Job two: Serve to the proper place

The angle of return allowed the receiver is critical to holding serve in doubles. A wide serve opens up the court for the receiver to return the ball at a sharp angle or down the alley past the net player. In the deuce court, a serve to the backhand or to the middle of the court keeps the court closed and enables the net player to poach effectively to help the server hold serve.

In figure 16-2, SD shows the best place to serve in the deuce court. In the ad court, the server might be concerned with a serve to the middle because the receiver (if right-handed) gets to hit a forehand. A serve wide to the backhand still makes the alley vulnerable, and enables a sharp angle cross-court return. For the best serve into the ad court, the server should aim at the receiver's left leg (SA in figure 16-2). The angles are kept closed, and the receiver's stroke is jammed. A wide serve can be used effectively, but it must be used with the correct timing. Although some aces will be hit, in doubles the primary purpose of the serve is to set up the second shot. Smart placement of the serve makes holding serve much easier.

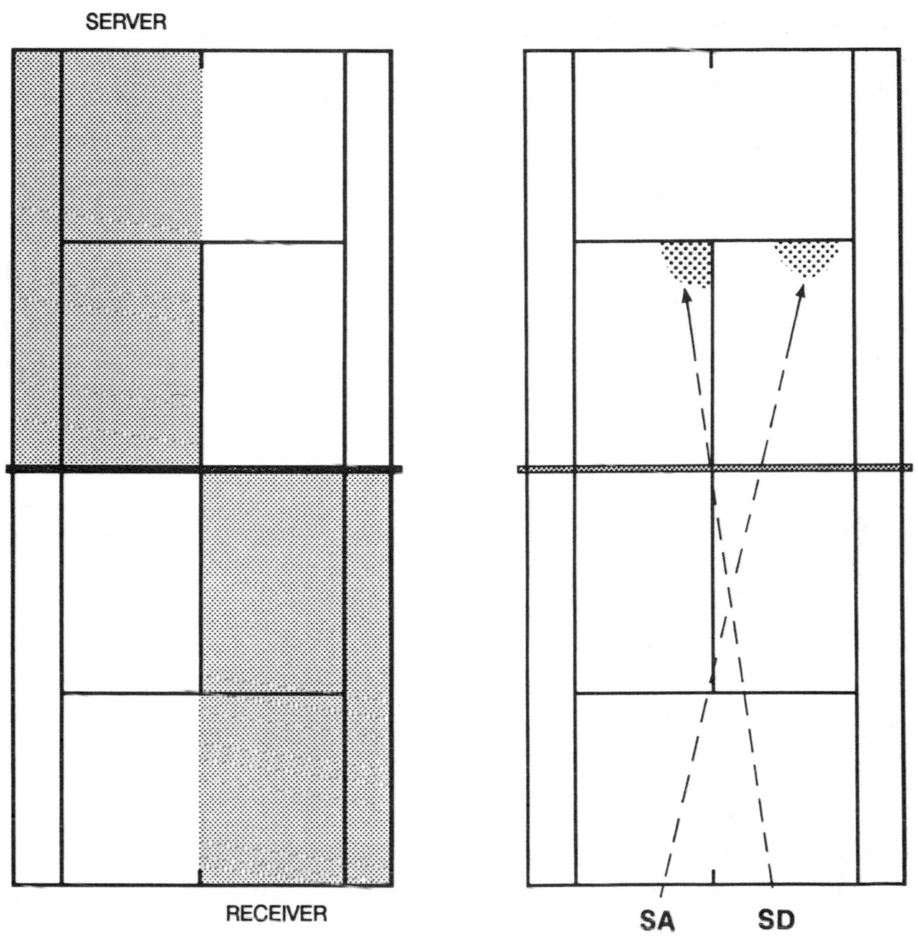

Figure 16-1.

Figure 16-2.

Job three: Place the first volley

For the same reasons that a wide serve should not be used very often, the first volley should not be angled unless it can be hit for a winner.

A first volley to the middle keeps the angles closed and prevents the receiving team from making an offensive shot. If the first volley is close enough to the middle of the court, the receiver will probably lob, which is what two players on the serving team would favor (see figure 16-3).

Job four: Get close to the net

The difference between hitting an offensive or a defensive first volley is the server's positioning close to the net. An offensive or put-away volley is possible on high returns if the server can move in quickly. A low ball will have to be dealt with more conservatively.

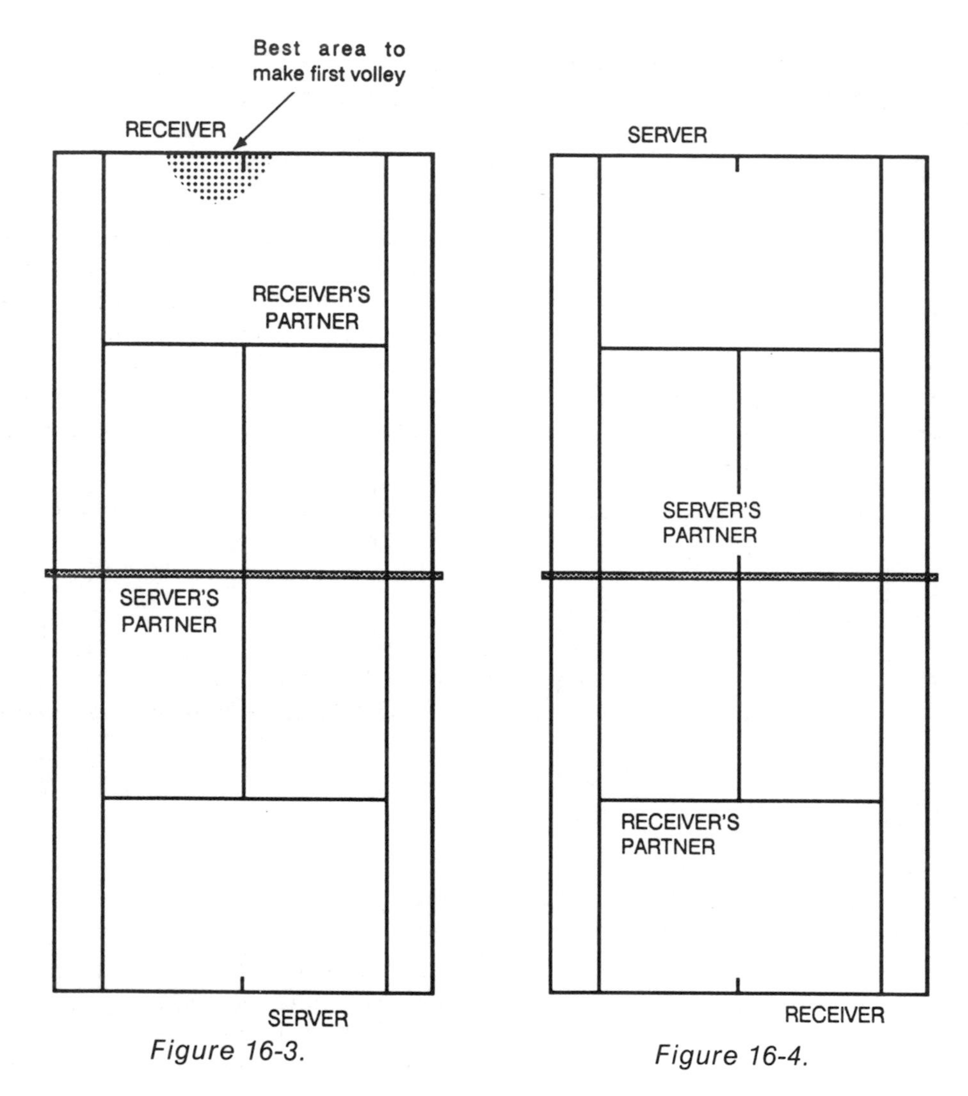

Figure 16-3.

Figure 16-4.

Job five: The server's responsibility

Poor communication between the server and partner often causes a break of serve. The most common scenario is when the server's partner starts to poach on a floating ball at the net and then changes his or her mind, leaving the server unready to make the volley and angry with the partner for not taking the ball. This only has to happen once for the server's partner to become either tentative or overly aggressive the next time in trying to make things happen.

Poor communication can be prevented with this rule: unless a planned poach is called, the server is responsible for all first volleys. If the server's partner rushes across with a swing and a miss, the server can still back up the play. This allows the poacher at the net total freedom to attack any ball that floats, increasing the chances of making a point-winning shot. The partner should cut off any reachable ball at the net, but the server is still available to play the first volley. The responsibility for all first volleys also places a healthy amount of pressure on the server to hold serve.

Job six: Use the I formation

The I Formation (sometimes called the Australian Formation) can be used as an excellent tactic when a receiver is in a groove and not missing many returns. Even if this formation does not result in missed returns, it will at least alter the returning player's groove and perhaps dampen the returning team's confidence. The I Formation (see figure 16-4) forces the receiving team to change the direction of the ball on the return to go down the line instead of cross-court. This change of direction usually causes errors on the service return.

One seldom-noticed advantage of the I Formation is the possibility of handcuffing the receiver's partner and preventing poaches.

It is important on service placement to realize that a wide serve enables the receiver an angle to hook the ball down the line, pinning the net player of the serving team. It is best to serve to the opponent's body, but the serve to the middle of the court also can work well. The I Formation should be practiced often so that the doubles team is comfortable with it in pressure situations.

The Receiver's Jobs

Job one: No returns wide or in the net

The basic responsibility of a player returning serve is to hit the ball over the net and through the opponents. The receiving player should ignore the poacher, and try not to change the direction of the return to reduce the possibility of an error. The rule is basic, but it should be ingrained in the player's subconscious. A ball hit wide or in the net is an immediate loss of the point. Most returning errors in doubles are the result of trying too hard to make a good shot. The player's "regular stuff" is good enough, as long as the rule "No balls wide, no balls in the net" is followed.

Job two: Determine strategy

Option one: Move into the net after returning a weak serve. Controlling the net is a great advantage in doubles, and when a receiver can take the net away from the serving team, it becomes easier to break serve. The return does not have to be hit hard, only deep into the court so the point can be won on the next volley. If the serve is weak, the receiver's partner also must be sure to move in.

Option two: Return the ball low at the server's feet, enabling your partner to cross for a winning poach. This is an advanced play that can be used effectively with the combination of a good returner and a good volleyer as the receiver's partner. The idea is to hit low and aggressive returns that force the server to pop up the first volley. The receiver's partner can intimidate the server by leading the server to press and make errors at critical times in the match.

Option three: Both players on the receiving team can play back and try to take the net off of the first weak ball. Dan Magill, tennis coach at the University of Georgia, used this formation exclusively. I seldom used it until his team defeated mine with this style at the 1986 NCAA Championships.

The objective is to take the pressure of making a great cross-court return every time off of the receiver. With both returning players back, the serving team has difficulty putting away the first volley. As soon as the first volley is made, the receiving team hits through the serving team until the serving team pops up an easy ball that makes for an easy winner for the receiving team. The offensive top-spin lob also is used occasionally to keep the serving team from closing too tightly to the net. The serving team gets its share of winners, but still makes many errors from being forced to handle so many volleys.

This formation takes practice, but if mastered it can beat opponents who are not good volleyers. The best doubles teams, though, usually will beat a defensive doubles team that uses this formation. Top-flight doubles is won at the net and players should definitely learn offensive tactics. The optimum would be to use the both-players-back receiving formation at strategic times.

The Server's Partner's Jobs

Job one: Direct the placement of serve

Much as a catcher does in baseball, the net player can give a signal that dictates the type or the placement of the serve. This is a very simple strategy that helps hold serve. If the server is directed to serve to the middle, the partner knows to move a step toward the middle with or without the fake of a poach. Other combinations also can be used.

Directing the serve with signals works better than calling poaches with signals because after the poach is called, the net player is forced to cross even if the server has hit a poor serve. When the placement of the serve is planned, the server's partner can watch for that specific serve and react accordingly. Poaches still can be planned, but they should be called verbally to avoid breakdowns in communication. To be effective, signals must be kept simple and specific.

Job two: Proper starting position

The starting position should be a position that enables the net man to move quickly on any floating ball. The weight should be on the inside foot, and the net player should be positioned a step or two farther back to be able to lean in as the receiver makes contact with the ball.

Job three: Attack floating balls

The net player to move on any ball that floats. This aggressive play often takes the receiver's concentration off making a solid return and helps score many points for the serving team. If the server's partner is tentative and does not move, the receiver has a great opportunity to get into a groove on the return. The already-stated rule for the server to assume responsibility for every first volley enables the net player to aggressively hunt floating balls.

Job four: Poach with lateral movement

Poaching with sideways or lateral movement gives the net player good balance to react to a ball that might be hit to an awkward position. The poacher often makes the mistake of running through a poach out of balance instead of moving laterally for the poach.

Job five: Stay aggressive at the net

The server's partner should not stand still, but should fake or cross. The job of the player at the net is to distract the concentration of the receiver through aggressive play; this greatly assists the effort to hold serve. Even making eye contact with the receiver can sometimes help tremendously. The server's partner should look for, and poach on, any floaters. If nothing else, the partner should draw fire from the receiver.

The Receiver's Partner's Jobs

Many players do not recognize the importance of the receiver's partner. If this position is played well, however, it can make for the difference between a good and a great doubles team. The receiver's partner has specific jobs in helping to break service.

Job one: Proper positioning

If the receiver's partner is at the service line, the partner can:

- Help make the service line call.
- Stay out of the way of the return of serve.
- Most importantly, react to a poach from the net player.

The receiver's partner should start out facing the opposing net player, because the opposing net player has the first play on the ball after the return. This allows the best opportunity to negate a poach through the middle. After the ball has been returned past the net player, the receiver's partner should take care of the next job.

Job two: Close off the net

Immediately after the ball is returned past the net player, the receiver's partner should take three steps straight in to close off the net. This puts pressure on the server's first volley and enables the receiving team to take advantage of a good return of service. Remaining at the service line only leaves the receiving team in a crippled situation.

Job three: Inside-inside or outside-outside coverage

After the receiver's partner has closed off the net, the partner should be focused on the server's first volley. If the ball is returned low and to the inside of the court, the receiver's partner should move to the inside lane to cut off the first volley. This puts tremendous pressure on the server's first volley. The server can try to hook a backhand volley from the inside to the outside behind the poaching receiver's partner. This forces the server to change the direction of the first volley that often leads to the serving team's errors at critical times in the match. If the receiver's return goes to the outside or to the server's forehand, the outside or line always must be covered.

Job four: Play back for a different look

As explained earlier, it is often a good tactic for both players to stay back for a different look to the servers. This should be done at strategic times according to the type of pressure the serving team needs to have put on them.

Picking a Partner

Before choosing a partner, it is important to understand what makes a good doubles team. The professional ranks have provided countless examples of two fairly good players who combined to make a great team.

A good doubles team should include a player who can attack and put balls away (the hitter) and a partner who makes few errors (the setter). The setter enables the hitter to play his or her style, and the hitter provides the element of recklessness and aggression that the setter cannot. Two setters together would fall prey to a more aggressive or a more consistent team, whereas two hitters on the same team would be hot or cold, either scoring great wins or very bad losses. The combination of a good hitter and a good setter works well if the two players get along with each other.

The personalities of the doubles partners also should complement each other. Two aggressive personalities do not work well together because they might end up fighting. Two passive personalities usually cannot make up their minds. Although neither personality must be overbearing, a comfortable mesh between them works well.

Who plays which court?

The decision of who should play the ad court and who should play the deuce court is based on who returns best in each court. The best returner should play the ad court, because that is where most of the big points are played. Except when the score is 40-15 or 15-40, games are won or lost in the ad court. Positioning the better returner in the ad court helps keep the pressure on a serving team and hopefully leads to a service break.

What about a left-hander?

A left-hander usually adds an extra dimension to a team's effectiveness. The left-hander's shots provide different spins and variety for the opponents.

Although some teams prefer to have a lefty play the ad court for cross-court returns, my preference is that the lefty play the deuce court, allowing both player's forehands to be in the middle for ground strokes and for poaching. Of course, both players must be able to handle the wide serve to the backhand well.

Movement and Tracking

It is often said that two players moving well as a doubles team appear as if they are connected invisibly as they move in unison.

Tracking, or the ability to cover the opponent's possible shots at the net, can be done effectively by following the rules of inside-inside/outside-outside. If your shot goes to the outside (your opponent's forehand in the deuce court or your opponent's backhand in the ad court), you or your partner must cover the potential outside shot, with the other player moving to cover the middle lane. The sharp cross-court angle is not the priority, because it is such a difficult shot to make. This outside-outside rule should force the opponents into trying this type of low percentage shot.

The rule for shots to the inside, or to the middle of the court, is that both players lean toward the middle with less attention given to the shot from the middle of the court to the outside. Figures 16-5 and 16-6 show inside-inside/ outside-outside coverage at the net.

These same rules apply to any situation where both players are at the net. Drills should be done with two players up and two back, or all four players up, to practice good teamwork in tracking and coverage.

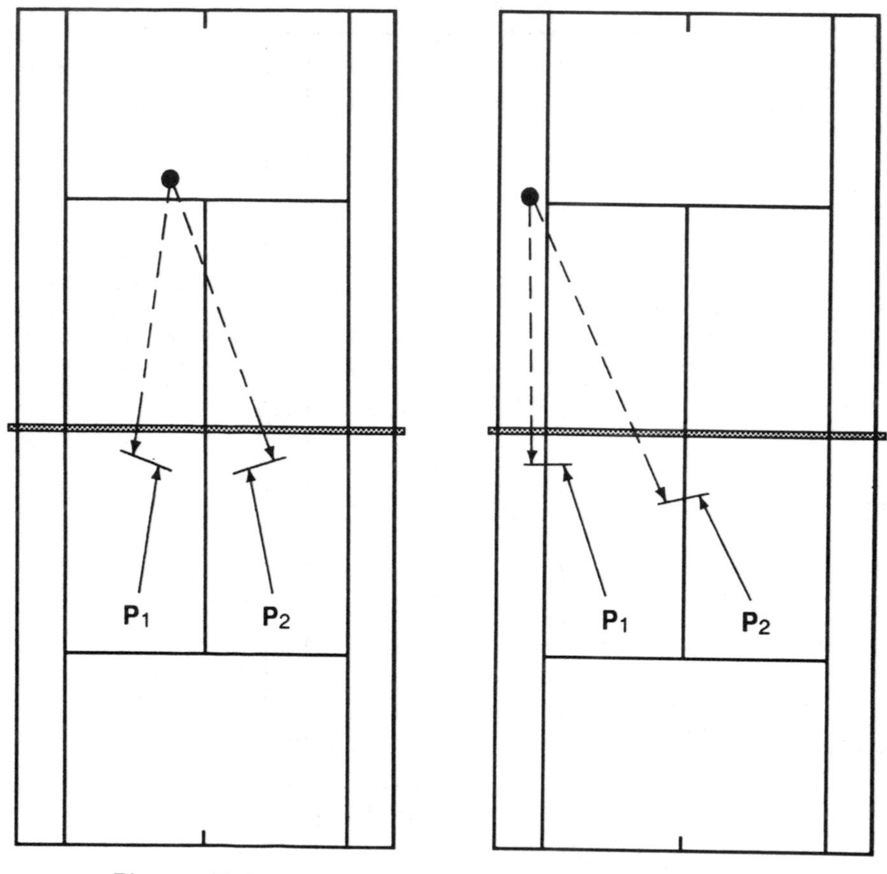

Figure 16-5. *Figure 16-6.*

Other important points of doubles play are as follows:

- Control the net and you will control the match. This is almost always true. With two players covering shots, it is hard to put balls away without taking the net. Work as a team in closing off the net.
- Go down the middle to set up your partner. A cross-court shot from the baseline against two net players is like a shooting gallery for them. A down-the-middle shot, if kept low, usually sets up a player's partner.
- Good positioning, not great shots, wins most often in doubles.
- Hit to the middle of the court on any ball that cannot be angled off for a winner. Remember that an angled shot opens up the court for your opponent's offensive shot.
- Hit through your opponents, not around them. This simply means that good doubles teams do not go for great shots, they keep angles closed while working to gain better positioning on the net.
- *Move, move, move,* and *close, close, close* for better court positioning.

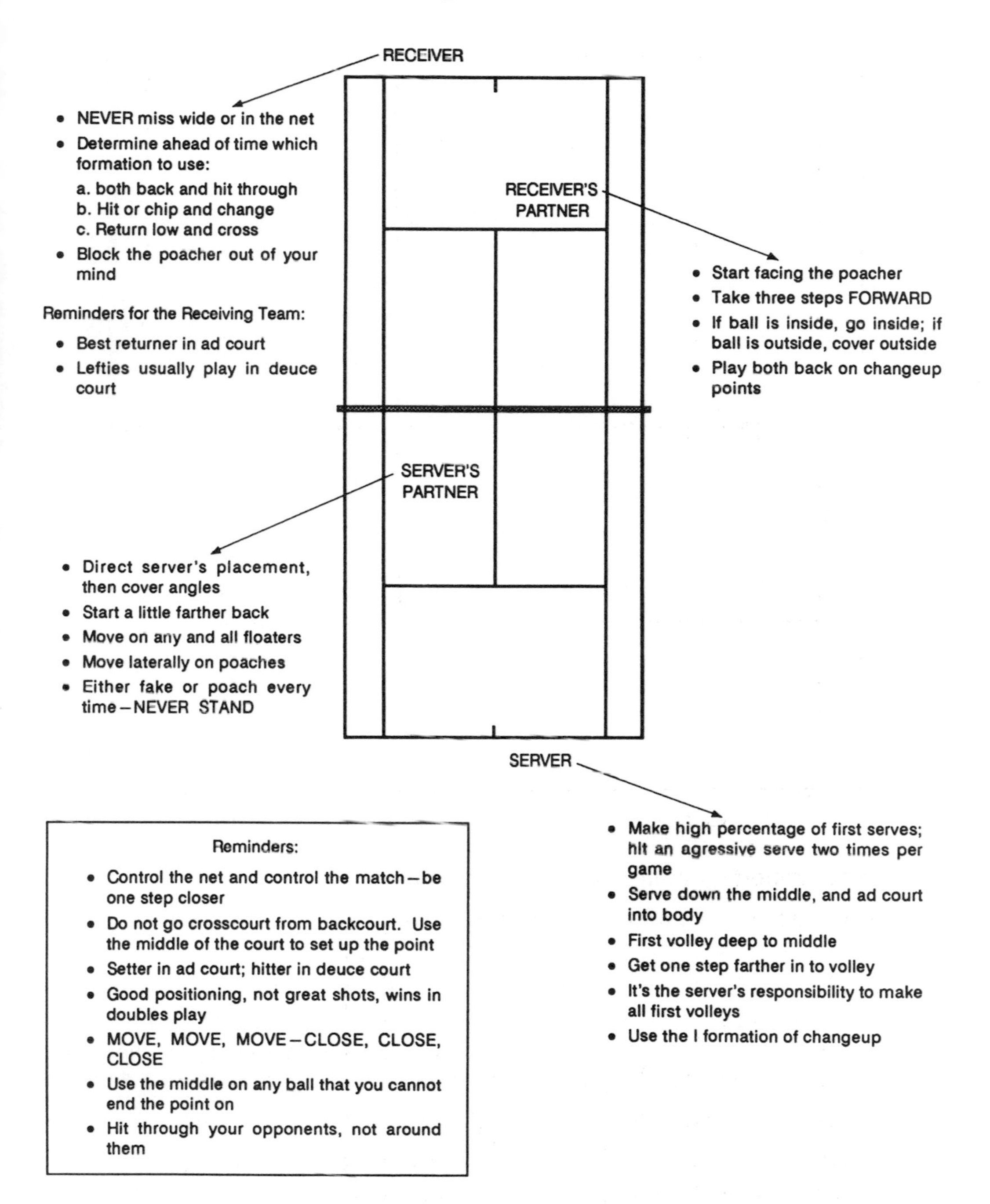

Figure 16-7. Doubles play — your role at each position.

Glossary

ACE — A serve hit so well that the opponent cannot touch it with the racquet.

AD — Short for advantage, the point after deuce. If it's the server's ad, the score is "ad in," if it's the receiver's ad, the score is "ad out."

ADVANTAGE — The next point after deuce.

ALLEY — The 4½-foot area that widens on each side of the court for doubles play.

AMERICAN TWIST — A severe top-spin serve that produces a high, sharp bounce after hitting the court.

APPROACH SHOT — The transition shot that a player follows to the net.

AUSTRALIAN FORMATION — Term sometimes used for the tandem or "I" formation, in which the server's partner lines up on the same side of the court as the server.

BACKCOURT — The area of the court between the service line and the baseline.

BACKSPIN — The spin created by hitting a ball with a high-to-low stroke.

BASELINE — The line that marks the boundary of the court farthest from the net.

BASELINE GAME	Style of play in which a player stays in the backcourt.
BREAK OF SERVE	To win the game that the opponent served.
BYE	An opening in the draw that enables a player to advance to the next round without playing a match.
CENTER SERVICE LINE	The line that separates the two service boxes on each side.
CENTER STRAP	Two-inch-wide, three-foot-high strap that holds down the net in the center.
CHOKE UP	To move the hand up on the racquet to make it lighter or more easily handled.
CHOP	A sharp downward stroke producing heavy back-spin.
COUNTER-PUNCHER	A player whose style of play emphasizes reacting to the other player's shots.
CLOSED TOURNAMENT	An event open only to members of a particular group or area.
CONTINENTAL GRIP	A grip halfway between the Eastern forehand and Eastern backhand grip, used for volleying and serving.
CROSS-COURT SHOT	A shot hit diagonally from one corner of the court diagonally to the opposite corner.
DEFAULT	A match won because the opponent did not show up to play or was disqualified.
DEUCE	When the score is tied with each player having won a minimum of three points each.
DEUCE COURT	The right court on one's own side of the net, and the left court on the other side of the net.

DOUBLE FAULT — Losing a point by two consecutive missed serves.

DOUBLES — A match played with two people on each team, four players total.

DOWN-THE-LINE SHOT — A shot hit parallel to the side line.

DROP SHOT — A ball hit barely over the net, forcing the opponent to run forward to make a play.

EASTERN GRIP — A "shake-hand grip" most commonly used for the forehand. The "V" between the thumb and index finger are on top of the racquet grip, with the racquet face perpendicular to the ground.

FAULT — A serve that misses the proper service box.

FIFTEEN — The score after winning one point in a game.

FOOT FAULT — When the server's foot touches or crosses the baseline or the center hash mark.

FOREHAND — Any shot hit on the right side of the body for a right-handed player or the left side for a left-handed player.

FORTY — The score after winning three points in a game.

GAME — A player wins a game by winning a minimum of four points, by a margin of two points. A minimum of six games must be won to win a set, by a margin of two games.

GRAND SLAM — Winning the Australian Open, French Open, U.S. Open and Wimbledon in the same year.

GROUND STROKE — Hitting the ball after it has bounced.

HALF-VOLLEY Hitting the ball immediately after it has hit the ground and is rising.

INVITATIONAL TOURNAMENT An event open only to a select group, by invitation.

I.T.F. International Tennis Federation.

KILL SHOT A shot hit so hard or placed so well that the opponent cannot reach it.

LET An interference, such as a distraction from the crowd, that causes the service or the point to be replayed.

LET SERVE A serve that hits the top of the net before landing in the service box; it is replayed.

LOB A high shot, made defensively to regain court positioning or offensively to clear the reach of the opponent at the net.

LOVE A score of zero.

MATCH A tennis contest, singles, doubles or mixed doubles, and usually consisting of two-out-of-three or three-out-of-five sets.

MATCH POINT The final point needed to win the match.

MIXED DOUBLES A doubles match played by teams consisting of one male and one female each.

NET GAME Playing in the forecourt.

NO-AD SCORING Also called VASS scoring, for Van Allen Simplified scoring system, in which the fourth point ends the game whether or not a player is ahead by two points.

OVERHEAD A smash shot usually hit after the opponent lobs; the technique is similar to the service motion.

PASSING SHOT A shot used to place the ball past a player at the net.

POACHING The crossing at the net by a doubles player to pick off a shot meant for the partner.

POINT One unit of scoring.

PRO-SET An abbreviated way to score a match. Instead of playing the best two-out-of-three sets, the match consists of one set of eight or 10 games, with a margin of at least two games needed to win.

RALLY The exchange of shots after the serve.

RECEIVER The player who is not the server.

RETRIEVER A player that plays a defensive style, focusing on returning all shots.

SERVICE The shot that initiates a point.

SERVICE BREAK When the server loses the game.

SET A group of games. To win a set, a player must win at least six games, with a minimum advantage of two games. A set score does not go higher than 7-5, except in Davis Cup play or special events. At 6-all, a tie-breaker is played in most situations.

SET POINT The last point needed to win the set.

SIDE LINE The side boundary of the court for singles or doubles play.

SINGLES	A contest between one player on each side of the net.
SLICE	A shot hit with back-spin on the ball.
SMASH	A hard overhead shot.
SPIN	The rotation on the ball.
SPLIT SETS	When each player has won one set in a match, forcing the play of a third set.
TAPE	The canvas that covers the cable at the top of the net.
THIRTY	The score after winning two points in a game.
TIE-BREAKER	An abbreviated scoring system used if the score reaches 6-all in a set. The most common tie-breaker is the 12-point tie-breaker.
TOP-SPIN	The forward rotation put on the ball with a low-to-high stroking pattern.
U.S.T.A.	United States Tennis Association, the sport's governing body in the U.S.
VOLLEY	A shot in which the ball is hit out of the air before it bounces.
WESTERN GRIP	A grip usually used on high bouncing balls that makes it possible to hit heavy top-spin.
WIDE	A shot landing outside of the side line boundary.

Bibliography

Bass, Ruth U. "An Analysis of the Components of Tests of Semi-circular Canal Function and of Static Dynamic Balance." *Research Quarterly* May 1939:33.

Benjamin, David. *The ITCA Guide to Coaching Winning Tennis.* New York: Prentice Hall, 1988.

Cooke, Jane, *Who's Who in Tennis*, World Champion Tennis, Inc., Kingsport Press, Inc., Dallas, Texas. 1983

Chui, Edward. "Effect of Systematic Weight Training on Athletic Power." *Research Quarterly* October 1950:188-194.

Endres, John P. "The Effect of Weight Training Exercise Upon Speed of Muscular Movements." Masters Thesis University of Wisconsin, 1953.

Everett, Peter, and Virginia Skillman, *Beginning Tennis*, Wadsworth Publishing, Inc., Belmont, California. 1968

Fox, Edward L. and Donald K. Matthews. *Interval Training*. Philadelphia: W. B. Saunders Co., 1974.

Grawunder, Ralph and Marion Steinmann. *Life and Health*. 3rd. ed. New York: Random House, Inc., 1980.

Hoffman, Marshal and Gabe Mirkin, M.D. *The Sports Medicine Book*. Boston: Little, Brown and Co., 1978.

Hoyt, Creig, et. al. *Food for Fitness*. 6th ed. Mountain View, CA: World Publications and Bike World Magazine, 1978.

Johnson, Barry I. and Jack K. Nelson. *Practical Measurements for Evaluation in Physical Education*. Minneapolis: Burgess Publishing Co., 1969.

Kohler, Taibi. *Personality Types*. Kohler and Associates Processed Communication Managers.

Kraft, Steve and Connie Haynes. *The Tennis Player's Diet*. New York: Doubleday and Co., Inc., 1975.

Lisciandro, Frank. *The Sugar Film*. Santa Barbara, CA: Image Associates, 1980.

Loehr, Jim. *Mental Toughness* (Video), 1989.

Masley, John W., Ara Hairabedian, and Donald N. Donaldson. "Weight Training in Relation to Strength, Speed, and Coordination." *Research Quarterly* October 1953:308-315.

Moore, Clancy, and M. B. Chafin. *Tennis Everyone*, Hunter Publishing Company, Winston-Salem, NorthCarolina. 1979.

O'Xendine, Joseph B. "Emotional Arousal and Motor Performance," *Quest* 13:23-31, 1970.

Sprague, Ken. *The Athlete's Body*. Los Angeles: Jeremy P. Tarcher, Inc., 1981.

Talbert, Bill and Pete Axthelm. *Tennis Observed*, Barre Publishers, Barre, Maryland. 1967

Wilkin, Bruce M. "The Effect of Weight Training on Speed of Movement." *Research Quarterly* October 1952:361-369.

United States Tennis Association, The, *The Illustrated Guide to the Rules of Tennis*, USTA Publications, Princeton, New Jersey. 1985.

Zorbas, William S. and Peter Karpovich. "The Effect of Weight Lifting Upon the Speed of Muscular Contraction." *Research Quarterly* May 1951:145-148.

About the Author

The numbers speak volumes for Chuck Kriese. So do the words.

Since taking over as head men's tennis coach at Clemson University in 1975, his teams have consistently ranked among the best in the nation. They compiled a 96-3 record in conference matches from 1978-'91, and they have won 10 conference championships and competed in the NCAA tournament 12 times. He has coached 27 All-Americans, and 14 of his players have gone on to play professionally.

That's only part of the story, however. Kriese is widely recognized as one of the top educators and motivators in his profession. He is an international speaker, and has appeared on ESPN's "Play Your Best Tennis" series. He also has coached the U.S. Junior Davis Cup team, the U.S. Sunshine Cup team, and was named the national Coach-of-the-Year by the ITCA in 1981 and by the USPTA in 1981 and '86.

Jay Berger, an All-American under Kriese, as well as a former U.S. Davis Cup Team member and current professional, says, "I learned a lot about motivation and intensity from Coach Kriese, and these skills help me now when I have to respond to tough situations in my professional matches."

Those who read this book, beginner and veteran alike, will benefit too.

MASTERS PRESS

DEAR VALUED CUSTOMER,

Masters Press is dedicated to bringing you timely and authoritative books for your personal and professional library. As a leading publisher of sports and fitness books, our goal is to provide you with easily accessible information on topics that interest you written by the most qualified authors. You can assist us in this endeavor by checking the box next to your particular areas of interest.

We appreciate your comments and will use the information to provide you with an expanded and more comprehensive selection of titles.

Thank you very much for taking the time to provide us with this helpful information.

Cordially,
Masters Press

Areas of interest in which you'd like to see Masters Press publish books:

☐ COACHING BOOKS
Which sports? What level of competition?

☐ INSTRUCTIONAL/DRILL BOOKS
Which sports? What level of competition?

☐ FITNESS/EXERCISE BOOKS
- ☐ Strength—Weight Training
- ☐ Body Building
- ☐ Other

☐ REFERENCE BOOKS
what kinds?

☐ BOOKS ON OTHER
Games, Hobbies
or Activities

Are you more likely to read a book or watch a video-tape to get the sports information you are looking for?

I'm interested in the following sports as a participant:

I'm interested in the following sports as an observer:

Please feel free to offer any comments or suggestions to help us shape our publishing plan for the future.

Name ______________________________ Age __________

Address ____

City ____________________ State __________ Zip __________

Daytime phone number ________________________________